NOTHING

THATO
MOTCHELLO

First Printing: 2015
ISBN 978-0-620-64685-7
Copyright © 2015 by Thato Motchello
motchello@gmail.com

ACKNOWLEDGEMENT AND DEDICATION

I would like and love to use this opportunity that I have right now to thank every single one person who has this Nothing in their hands right now. Thank you for reading this, thank you for laughing with me, thank you for listening, feeling and sharing with me in this way.
Thank you for being there for me, thank you for everything and thank you for Nothing.

I love you all.
I love each and every single one of you.
There is Nothing to do but to love you all in this way I do right now, here, there and then and everywhere now!
Finally I would like to thank me. Because after reading this, I now understand.
I Understand.

ABOUT THE AUTHOR

You are the author of this book.

This book is about the person who is holding it now.

I was born and raised in a small little town, and a big and huge city of this state or province in this country. I was very happy in my early childhood days as a young being because I had nothing to do, no responsibilities and no worries at all but just to play around and be myself the way I knew myself to be as a child.

Things started to change when I grew youthful, and all of a sudden I had responsibilities, I had things to account to for my living that I never had before. I had to wake up early in the morning to be at an Educational Institution that will show me, and teach me how to be responsible for the things I am responsible for. The institution had a role in my life, and the role was for it to remind me how to be responsible for my life. I began reading books, the institution taught and showed me how to write, how to speak and talk, how to have safe and unsafe sex, how to respect and how not to respect people, how to be a bully and violent, how to be loving and understanding, how the universe works, it also taught me about God, and how to walk properly and how not to do the things I was doing before when I was still a child, how to always dream and reach my goals and never give up on my dreams, and I also fell in love at the institution and with the institution.

After I had finished with the institution of learning, I went to another Educational Institution and a Job Institution at the same Time. The role of the Job Institution, was to help me be that which I dream to be by paying me money to achieve my dreams. After some time and long hard work, I saw that I was going nowhere slowly, and I still had not gotten to my dreams after all this time. I was now sad, lonely and confused, I was looking and searching for my dreams that I was taught to follow in the Educational Institution.

After all that life drama, I then decided to follow no dreams at all but my own now dreams. And my dream right now is to help me find myself, to find my true dreams. And this is why I wrote this, and my name is on the next flipped page.

That is who I am. And this is my name.

My name is Thato Motchello. I am writing these notes now at this moment because my mind, body, soul, thought and spirit have gone weary of searching for that which is truth in human reality and my own personal experience. Daily, and momentarily I do not cease to contemplate on what is the truth, and on how to make the most of my life. I may not have browsed or read through many books, but what I have read seems to be enough because most books are related in one way or the other. I would like to admit that most or least for that matter, of the books that I have read are of consciousness, science, spirituality, and secrete doctrines of cult and religion. I never got the hang of reading financial and personal gain of or for money or how to be rich books. I guess or would assume that I have always seen no need of or for money although I am consciously and unconsciously using it. However, my curiosity is mostly of how powerful a person or human beings are. So then, most or at least of these books that I have read were motivated by what is written in the bible, mythology or religious doctrines. So I later lost interest in reading books because they all had and have the same questions and quest of who God is, and all never give the answers. So then it was that I ended up finding similar myths through most if not all the material that I have gone through of all different cultures and individuated societies of race and colour.

Then again one would ask why do I not read financial gain and money books or how to be rich books? The answer to this question would be quick and easy, let me make an example. Do you not think that if you read a book on how to be the best market trader, or on how to be rich and gain wealth, that the very same book will trigger anxiousness and curiosity of you reading another book that is in line or the same context as the first one that you read? Or even reading another one different from the other? Well for sure it will, and all of it will lead to one ultimate similar foundation and some relation here and there. The truth is that some books may be thoroughly explained... a person would say that the other one particular book is better than the other one, but it is not. It is merely the same book, just with more explanation and meaning to what you read from the first book. Hence some people who come across the more thoroughly explained book at first, and then read other books after the first one would argue that, what they read at first is better than the rest because all has been detailed and well explained in the book that he or she read at first.

My mind or thoughts I should say, tell me now in this moment that I do not have to be hasty on writing these notes because I have all the time I have ever needed. There is no need to be quick at this because I am not writing for or to someone but me. So then, everything that shall be digitally inked on this paper, that is to say my thoughts, but very most importantly my feelings will not be written down all at the same time, but all will be written in one moment. The purpose of these notes is for me to refer back to me. As I refer back, I will be able to realize if I am still in the same alignment as what I have written down of who I am.

I would like to get right on to it now.
I feel and wish to experience pure pleasure, pure joy and pure love. I mean who does not? But my greatest desire is not to work for that which I wish for. I wish for the absence of need, I would like to be anywhere at any given moment, do what I please at any given moment, eat what I choose at any given moment... then again who does not? I would love to be myself, even as I say to be myself, I feel so confused of who I am... indeed who am I? Am I you the reader or any other next person? What am I really? What are or is my utmost capability, what can I really be? What can my body achieve? What makes me as a human and why do I feel that I am greater than that which I am now?
Why, why, why?
Well this is the whole point and purpose of why these notes are written down hey. They are to answer the questions that I have asked above through my daily experiences, feelings and thoughts.

I really do not know where to start, but then again I do not need to know, all I have to do is just to start.
First I will ask myself this question. Why would I like to live without need, why should I even be without need, why should there be need to feel to be without need? Now this is a very big question, it so huge that it is confused and misunderstood. So I warn myself beforehand that there will be some contradictions, but then again the whole point is to give answers to what seems to be difficult and contrary to itself.

This is my answer, this is what I think and feel. Well because I know one thing for sure, and that is I am birthed without need.

Before I continue, a thought has come to mind or mind has come to thought. It tells me therefore what I am saying is that, if I am birthed without a need, then I do not need to eat right?
I am aware that without food, there is starvation and after starvation there is what we as humans call death. But then again science speculates that a person can go on without food, for not more than one month if not less. And also it speculates that a person can go on without water for at maximum a week. The question then arises, who has dared to go for three months without food or water? Who has dared to go for a year without food or water? I know of none nor have I even tried a week. Then that means I need to eat right?

But then again somehow there is greater sense of feel that I do not need. My mind paints a picture of all life, plants, animals, water, sun, moon, earth as whole and everything in the universe. A picture is clearly painted that life gives life to live. At first I am not birthed or created in this state of form I know myself to be as human, or at least I think so. And then I became born in to life as life. I am in this state of being of life, and from life I take to develop this one particular form of being of life. Therefore if I am life and life is giving me food, then I do not need food because I am life. Now life gave birth to me to take from life itself for this particular current state of being as itself. However since life gave birth to me, I am dependent on life and life not on to me.

I still feel confused, and I feel for and think for more clarity on this matter. I have the thoughts which I have turned in to written words, but still, I have not fully understood what I just wrote down now.
If life gave me life, then it is not possible for me to take from life, because the act of taking from life that has given life to me, means that by taking I am giving to what life has produced, which is me. Let me give or make a simple example by asking a question, actually it is not much of an example but is what is.

Now then, since I think to know that I do not need to eat but do think that I need to eat. What do I think happens or has happened to all the water I have drank, to all the food I have eaten and to all the air I have breathed? Where has it all gone to, all that food and water that I thought I so much needed all these years and cannot live without? Where is all the intake stored at that which I have consumed and stressed so much of?

Now that is a good interesting question, and the truth is that it is so simple it does not even need much thinking. I know that when I drink water or eat food, it goes in my body and it is stored for a while, until there comes a time again for me to take the very same water, and or food I have drank or ate in to my body system out. So now this clearly indicates to me without doubt that what I have taken from the earth which is water and or food goes back through me. It is like I am a small river or stream that only channels a fraction of what is flowing through. Well science would tell and explain all the chemical and molecular processes involved in the system process, but I am only keeping it simple to my own observed understanding of what I see.

My second thought tells me not to confuse need with what should be done. I do not know what I want. What should I do? One moment I have it all together, I am the great Mr. I know it all, then at one time it all seems to be fading away from me. Like I know I should have gone to college or work and submitted some of my project but I did not.
After feeling guilty for not submitting and feeling down with myself and all the emotional breakdown, my thoughts think of the future, how to better my life and what I will be or do after college or work, and do I even need to better my life? The question would then be am I happy now? If I am or at least think that I am, then I should listen to my deepest voice that I have always known myself to have or be.

I want to be given an idea of what to do, and then again I don't want to be given an idea of what to do and how to run my life. How do I escape this life I have indulged in for so long? What do I choose, and why is it taking so long on acquiring that which I choose and wish for? Why not have it all now? Yes I know that I could have it all now. But how do I touch it, How do I feel it?

What is it that I really want?

Or what is it that I really do not want?

Well, I know for sure that:

I hate long school attendance.

I do not enjoy working, especially lately.

I just want and feel to do what I choose without going through to do what I do not want.

Ahhhhhhhh…. Who is there to help me, can anyone hear me now! Oh, ooohh the deep aches of heart, mind and spirit, I love you. I do not know to whom am I telling that, but I feel to just say it. Yes, I love you with all my heart. Please do not leave me, be with me now and forever more. Guide me, be true way of my true path. Let my imagination pave and paint it clearer for me with your help. Hear me now as I come to you. Help me realize who I am and what I am. I ask for mighty strength. I have never done it alone, although I would like to think that have at most times. You are the pillar of my heart and true divinity, show me compassion. Show me love, true love that I am. Let me be the source of help and shelter with guidance for others.

Oh, my father, oh my mother I so long for you. Touch me, be smooth to me, and be gentle to me. Screams and shouts are in my head. Voices of torment are calling out. Where is it all coming from, where do I escape to? Let light shine and be the guider and let darkness let light to be.

Mmmhhhhh… I have let myself to my own now truth.

Yes indeed, you have let yourself to this now truth.

It has been a while since I am writing these notes about me and how to live and become the best of living life according to what I feel is arousing, pleasing and satisfyingly good to me. See, a lot has happened during the days of being absent from these notes, I went to be the experience of knowing in this form I know myself to be.

I would like to remind myself that I have not forgotten that I am still on the subject of solving… "need" and to be without need.

Yes, yes, yes, I have not forgotten yet. I just want to share some of my re-found truth that leads to the solution of hunger, struggle or need.

I must really say that I have all these answers or my own realized truth in my head. I am experiencing multiple thoughts and solution of all the questions I have always had or wanted to experience. I feel a bit fearful because my truth is near, and I also know for a fact that it is happening now.

Oh how good it is to know.
I feel free from the unknown and the known. The thoughts and imagination of my own led knowing truth is so pleasing, it gives me so much joy and relief. It keeps me at ease in the night for I now know. I feel so blessed to have met myself in this way. To be honest I have always felt and seen myself as a being with greatness. And I get to choose and decide how or what greatness part of me I take. The knowing is so sweet and tinkles, which makes me laugh because I am knowing. The word truth merely exists for I have made my own truth.
I have heard my own voice and I am hearing it now.
I have asked and caused myself to know, but what is to know?
What do I want to know?
That which I know, where does it come from?
It could be any kind or sort of knowing from anywhere.

I have realized that the truth has no lie and confusion in it. And a lie has no truth and has confusion in it.
The truth always leads to the truth, in most cases through a lie.
I can reject the truth, and if I reject what is true I am opting for what is not true. By choosing what is not true, my life and the things I will be doing will be based on a lie yet at the same time I become the truth about that lie. I become a testimony of lie. In a sense I should say I become a true lie. You see it matters not whether I choose the truth, lie or true lie.
So then, if I feel confused and do not understand something or anything, it is to my own good to fully find out, know and understand why and how should it be that, that one particular thing or something should be the way it is until I am satisfied. Knowing can be understood through experiences of my own or someone's experiences or just simply by observing my space or surrounding.
I have realized that a lot of people do not know how to sleep dream. And by this I mean they really do not know how to sleep dream. One can ask,

6

but what do you mean that I do not know how to sleep dream? Well for instance I would like to ask a question which I already have the answer to. I say it is the answer because it makes me calm, it does not confuse me or lead me to more unclear answers and questions. And the question is, what do you think sleep is? Or what do you know dreams to be? When do you say I am asleep? Do I even know when I fall asleep?
Can you or I differentiate between sleep dream state and what you consider being awake?

Well my own answer is that I do not know how to sleep but I can sleep. Come, let us think of it this way, if I knew how to sleep dream I would sleep immediately and whenever I choose to right?
Well yes I would.
I should actually say that people do not know how to dream. A person can sleep and fall unconsciously or consciously into a dream state, and this kind of sleep is the sleep known as deep sleep or dream state.

Okay cool, now that we both know that I dream unconsciously or consciously, I would like you who is me, to imagine if you could sleep at own command of will. My truth is that you actually sleep at will. Anyway, let us imagine it **now then**. I will be interrupting myself in between any thoughts and words to write any new next thought or word as it comes to mind, and that appears to can best explain sleep and wakefulness and any other subject we are involved in with, here and now or then. When I read four lines back up. I realize that the words **now** and **then** are not joined but there is space between them. Which could, "could" mean that or suggest that now and then are one thing divided or split in to two. So I suppose that one could make sense of that line in this way. "Let us imagine it now then", this means that what you imagine now is already then as you imagine it now then. Or you could for instance say, "Then now what happened?"
Do you notice or see how things are happening or happened **now then**?
As it is happening now, so be it then.

This information is so good to me. I feel good energy that does not collide with itself to make terrifying impact which is known as negative energy. It is making me aware of the now then creation. I can see how now is

7

connected to then. For example, if I would or may start to dance or play soccer now at this moment, not thinking how to kick the ball or how to dance but just doing it now, I can see myself playing soccer then. But immediately I stop dancing or playing soccer now, then also stops and takes or changes the routine of or to what I am doing now. To explain this a bit more clearer to my best understanding, is to say I can imagine myself to be whatever I choose to be, whether it is being a dancer or soccer player now, and do it forever now then. This means that whatever I do **now** is reflected to **then**. And if now is perfected truly, truly it will be perfected then, and it will be noticed by those who are looking or observing. It is like doing the same thing every day and every minute moment without stopping being what you wish, and desire or choose. In fact it is like doing. Like is doing, since you do what you like and to like is to be or do like or choose not to do like.

I would like for you to look at this carefully, if you do not do like, you will not be like. Hence you find a little child liking a particular observation becomes or do what she or he likes or liked from observing like. The observation can be from a parent, friend, family member, stranger, the surrounding natural environment or television. So now, this means that you have to or should think and see what it is that you strongly feel and desire to become **now then**.

Phheeewww…. Okay.
Now let's go back to talking about dream state sleep.
Yes please Sir.

Now listen very carefully.
You do not know how and when to dream. Yes I do know that you can dream, but how do you find yourself in a dream? That is the question you should ask yourself.
I find myself in a dream when I am sleeping.
Good, we are getting closer.
When do you sleep?
I sleep anytime.
Yes, that is correct you do sleep at any given time.
Now I would like you to sleep and go into dream state now!
Ahhhhmmm… ahhhh… now?

8

Yes now! And I mean it as in now instantly.
I do not know how to do that.

See what I mean? You cannot go to sleep at own will unless you are feeling tired. Right now you think that you first have to feel tired or drowsy before you can fall asleep. Sleeping is one thing and getting to dream is another. For most of you it takes a while to sleep, once having gained sleep you now have to enter what you call dream state which takes a few more minutes before you can enter or fall into it as a dream as you think it to be. If you had the will to fall into dream state sleep instantly at any time you wish, you would do so now, but because you have so much believed one part to be true that you find the other part not true. Instead of looking at both parts as one and true, you have divided them. Thus you have called one part a dream and the other a reality. Instead of seeing both as a reality or dream, you have chosen to separate them. In truth they are one and they are connected. You are engaged in your dream here right then and now. You so much love this dream that you are in now that you spend a lot of time in it, and you do not see it. The more time spent in thy beloved dream, the more different things can be done in that one state of dream you know yourself or have created yourself to be. Yes, that is the truth. You can deny it and reject or accept it and realize it. Hhhhhmmmmmmhhh....
One of the simplest ways to explain this would be for you to start using your imagination now. This can be with your eyes open or closed whichever way you feel comfortable with is okay. Imagine if you could sleep and fall into dream state anytime you wanted and at will. What would you do? Would you choose to dream every second and moment of time? Even though you are doing it now, what kind of a dream would you visit? Think about the dream you had last night, yesterday, last week, last month or last year, think of any dream that you would like to re-visit. You can even think of a dream that you call your future dreams, the dreams that you say are your academics career or job. Where, what or which dream will you take? Will it be a nightmare, a dream with snakes, monsters, rapists, killers and or suffering? Or will it be a dream full of fantasies, riches of wealth and or magic? Do you wish to dream being a pilot? How long will you remain in that particular dream? After fulfilling its

purpose will you dream differently or come back to what you know now as reality?
What dream do you choose?
What do you choose?
And it is that easy, all you have to do is to choose!

But if all my realities are dreams or all my dreams are realities, for example. Then why when I dream or realize myself in a situation whereby experience death from a terrifying car accident only to find out that when I open my eyes I am still in a good condition and nothing has happened to me? And also why does the same dream re-occur as many times as I cannot remember?

Good, very good. I like your questions. I also like what you said when you said, "nothing has happened to me?" And that is the ultimate truth, Nothing is happening to you but for now we will stick to what you know. Well then, you see, the truth is that it has happened and it is happening now. It is there because it is a choice, and you get to choose it. But the biggest question is how many times will you re-visit that one same dream? What actually takes place is that you did experience death, yes you died already but because you are not happy with how you experienced your death, you keep on re-visiting your last good known condition or state before you died, which in most cases was on the bed sleeping. You keep doing this because you are trying to avoid, prevent or fix that which has occurred from happening. Also you will keep on re-visiting that one dream if you think too much about or of it, and that is because thinking is imagining.
Your friends, family relatives and what you call random strangers have asked you of what your dreams are? See the question itself is posed without understanding the true meaning of it. When someone asks you of your future dreams, they are simply asking you what you would like or wish to experience. Now that is the true meaning of a dream. You know this, all of you know this but the thought that dreams can only be achieved in the future has led you astray. You have to look at this from all angles that make up or form a circle. Therefore you should ask yourself what are dreams or what is a dream? As always the answer is very simple to this question, it only becomes difficult if you fail to grasp it.

Let me tell you this then, dreams are experiences, and experiences depends on desired choices, you get to choose what you like and experience and become like. And also you can experience what you do not like. Not like normally or most of the time happens when trying to figure out why you are experiencing what you do not like. Since you like, want and choose to figure out the experience of that one ugly experience that you do not like, you tend to spend a lot of time re-experiencing it. And in this case, what you like is to know how and why what you do not like keeps on happening? And in doing this you find different angles approach to a single experience. This is also one of the reasons why you keep on having the same nightmare or reoccurrences of one same dream. I know what confuses you Thato. Well you are not the only one who is confused. The good news is that you do not have to be anymore. What confuses many of you is the setting of dreams. You can dream being with a loved family member back at home in your family house, and within a split second you are at school and your mom is waving good bye to you, and just when you thought that was it, you are suddenly involved in an argument with your teacher in a class room. Everything seems to be everywhere at the same time. And the question would be why it is so? I tell you this, it is so because you do not have control of your dream state as compared to what you call your own reality. You have been in this side of your own reality for a long continuous repetitive moment of time because you choose and love this form of being that you call human. Instead of controlling your human reality you have given your will of experience to the creation itself.

Remember this son; your poverty is someone's riches, and your riches are someone's poverty. This means that what you consider as poverty and struggle, someone may envy it as success. And what you consider as riches or success, someone may see it as poverty or struggle. So then, you could be at the bottom and in the middle and top at the same time, in the end it matters not where you are and what others think. The only important thing would be if you are happy with what you have created and thought of or for yourself. It is about how comfortable you feel about yourself, condition and situation you are in and experiencing. Suffering therefore is experienced through a disliked re-occurring event. So then, are you happy now? If not, why not change it? Should you feel that you have tried everything and Nothing is working, why use the same method of approach? The most common fall in self-believe is to follow trend, which is to follow what others have created for themselves. And remember that what you like you create. This becomes a problem when like is not met. So if you observed something from someone or others, and you find it very strongly pleasing and likable to you, you will follow it or them and even believe it as you have liked it. And if all efforts of being like that one particular observation from someone or something fails, it is labeled failure or struggle because it is not met.

Thinking is a process to define and alter creation. Imagination is creation, to imagine something is to create it. When thinking is used very rapidly it alters and changes the entire imagined creation, and a new creation is thus therefore created within a creation and dual or multiple creations occurs within that very single creation. This is caused by not being aware of your creation or by being unpleased with it. Since you are unpleased or not aware with your creation, you start not to like it anymore and thus start to produce not like and to question why you ever created such a condition and state. If creation is unrecognized then confusion, anger and pain troubles the mind and body.
Why me?
What did I do?
Why is all of this happening to me?
What did I do to deserve all of this?
Does anyone, anybody or anything deserve all these things to happen to them or it?
What is the cause and who is to blame?
These are the questions that start to manifest when thinking is used. But if you use imagination or creation and recognize your own creation and set aside thinking, one starts to accept and know that he or she is responsible for what is or has occurred. This can be easily understood when one acknowledges that he or she has chosen to experience and share creation. By this I mean you come to realize that you are responsible for what you choose, and whatever choice you make you share it with someone's choice as well.

A shared thought of choice is also very difficult to can see, acknowledge and mostly to realize.

What is a shared thought of choice?

A shared thought of choice is a choice that you make to experience someone's choice of thought. If you choose to do something or one thing, know that someone is also making a choice with you at the very same moment of time to make your choice manifest, you are all sharing your thoughts of choice. Let's try to be practical with this. A taxi driver decides and chooses to wake up in the morning determine to make some money for himself by taking or driving people to their own desired destination. A student or a worker decides and chooses to wake up in the morning determine to get to college or work, and he or she wants or would like to be taken or driven by a taxi to his or her desired destination, and is willing to pay for it.

Now then, realize this.

You have two people with different choices. One choice is to get there, and that is the choice of a student or worker. Another choice is to take you there, and that is the choice of a taxi driver. So far we have two people with their own choices in the same time of morning deciding to realitize what they imagined doing. Now we are outside, the student or worker sees the taxi from a distance approaching, and the taxi driver also sees the student or worker from a distance approaching. Now then both parts or sides are aware of each other and they are filled with joy, anticipation and excitement because they now know that it is finally happening, they know that their choices of thought are happening. The student or worker raises a hand to signal the taxi driver before approach, and the taxi driver hoots or flashes to signal the student or worker before approach. The taxi stops and the student or worker gets in to the taxi.

"Hello Sir", says the student or worker.

"Hello to you too there. Where may I take you?" The driver said.

"I would like to be dropped off by St. Peters Square in Observatory, here is your fare", said the student or worker.

"Thank you", said the driver.

"No thank you", said the student or worker.

Now then, also realize this.

If the student or worker and the driver both realized instantly at that moment why they said, "thank you." to each other, they would both

actually say, "thank you for sharing your choice with me, thank you for making it happen. I am happy and you are happy that you chose this, in fact we chose this and this is all so beautiful what we have created here. Me and you created this beautiful journey, this beautiful moment, and I love it and I love you and we love each other!"
And that is how beautiful a student or worker met a taxi driver.

Wow that is a beautiful story.
Everything is beautiful. You are beautiful. All is beautiful and you are all of it. Without you, it will not be all of it because you made all of it.
So then, do you now understand how you share your choices with others? Do you now see how you relate with others just by making a choice?
Ahhhhmmm…. I think I do.
Good, do not forget it then, otherwise you will have to remember it.
I do not understand. Is it a bad thing to remember?
Nope, not at all, but then again why would you remember what you remembered?
What do you mean Thato?
Okay stay focused, pay attention and listen very well.
Okay I am ready. Let's do it.
Remember I told you that everything is beautiful and that you are beautiful?
Yes I do remember but I did not forget.
Good, did you have to remember what you know?
No. Unless I want to know what I remembered again, then yes.
You see, you are a beautiful magnificent big memory. That is who you are, you are indeed re-membering, re-connecting and re-joining pieces of memory together. So then, if you do not know something or anything, just remember it and you will know it again as you have remembered it. I say again because that is all that you are doing. You are just remembering what you know already. So then my son, wherever you are at any moment of time experiencing something that is anything; you should say ahhhh… bingo… I remember that I was here and that I did this once. So then my son, remember yourself. Remember yourself anywhere where you left yourself. Oh yes, you pretty much have left yourself everywhere and so far this is what you have remembered yourself to be doing or to have

become. And this is you and you are that, and that which is you, is one big beautiful magnificent memory. You are beautiful indeed.

Wow… wow… this is really good. I am enjoying this. I have never told myself that I love myself and that I am beautiful in this way. I feel appreciation of myself, and it brings a feel good feeling on to me. I love myself as an imagination and my imagination is in my memory. Do I even need to memorize this? Nope. Oh how much I love you Thato, yes… yes… yes I do love you. Since I love myself so much, I do not want to hurt or feel any pain of sort, may it be guilty, sad, chemical, physical or emotional. I do not want to experience all these things. I choose not to experience them because they are not good to my body of thought. Now then, since I have forgotten what is good for me, I choose to remember what is good to and for me. Now I choose to remember, and if I want to re-member I have to use my imagination and after using my imagination I am thus creating, after creating I will then choose my creation.

Now remember this.
Okay, I am listening.
You have made an observation of the day because of the sun. You have also realized that without the sun there is no day. You have come to recognize and appreciate that there is no day at all but only night. In order for a day to exist there had to be light, thus you have the sun. You were told in school that the earth moves around the sun and this new information to you encouraged you into knowing what you know differently from what you have observed. Very well then, now you know that the earth revolves the sun and you also know from your observation that the sun revolves the earth. You have two things here, and you know both.

So far you choose to know what you know and what you are or were told, and it is all good to know and be aware of this. So then let us take what you know and what you are or were told to know. Let us start with what you were told. You were told that the earth revolves the sun and at the very same time it is spinning. So now you have earth that is spinning and revolving, and in it being so, you were told how many times it spins and revolves the sun. So now since you know how many times the earth spins

and rotates the sun, you then decided to accept what you have been told as your own truth separate from what you already know and have observed. If you ask any scientist where does the earth rise? He or she will probably say… "ahhmmmm…. what kind of a question is that? What do you mean by where does the earth rise? The earth never rises, only the sun rises from east to west. Are you crazy or trying to be funny? I have never seen the earth rise accept for what I know."
And you may ask, "What do you know?"
Good, very good, and now we can start jumping to what you know and were not told but only observe from sight.

What you know is that the sun spins and rotates or revolves the earth, this is your truth and this is what you know. Now then since you know that earth rotates the sun and or the sun rotates the earth which ever outcome is, they both make or give rise to a day. Then after knowing that there is such a thing called day, you have broken it in to 24 revolutions of hours. Now you have, let us for now say two creations, a day and hours of the day.
Do you agree with what you are telling yourself so far?
Yes I do, yes I do agree, I am actually agreeing to my knowledge.
Good! All is good and you are all good.

Now then let's get right back to it.
Yes. Shall we?
Oh we are and we will now and then. Yes, so we have a day with twenty four hours. After creating a full day you then decide to break it again after completing it. Thus you have created day of the day and night of the day. Since one 24 hours of day split in to two is two parts, you called the other half of 24 hours a day, which is 12 hours of light day because this is the only time you can see and observe the sun that makes a day. You then took the other half of the same 24 hours, which is 12 hours of the very same day, and called it night because you could not see or observe the sun that makes up a day. Very well then, you made another great observation, you observed and realized that you can actually sleep when the sun is not seen from sight. Since the only time you could not see the sun was and is night time of the day, you decided to sleep during the night and do Nothing but sleep during that time of the whole now day time.

Oh my, what a great discovery this was to you. It is and was always astonishing for you to realize this. But then again this meant that you would have to keep up with the sun, and know when it rises. For some time you struggled to keep up with this because you did not know or in this case of you knowing yourself, I would say you did not remember it. Finally after a while you figured it out and decided not to sleep during the period of night of the day, and once you had it right, you chose to get it right as many times as you have now chosen to. For you to do this you developed ways of assisting you to waking up to sunrise, and one of your ways before was sounds of animals from your natural surrounding environment. After a while you got the hang of waking up to the sun, you did this as many times as you wished as you have and are doing it now.

You have remembered.

And now then, since you can control state of dream of night of the day and also control the state of wakefulness of day of day, you acknowledged that you can do whatever you choose. You even realized that you can sleep during the day, and thus do you sleep whenever you give yourself chance to sleep during the day of a day where or when there is sun. But still this is and was mind blowing for you. Your mind was and is so far off blown that when you realized it you started laughing for no reason. Very well then, since you know and knew how to sleep at own will, you decided to keep yourself busy by doing what you love mostly during day time, and you have loved everything so far. Yes I know you can think yourself not enjoying some moments, but that is because you allowed yourself to be and feel what you were and are feeling at that or this moment of time. But then again if I did not love and like what I felt at that or this time, why do I even do it or continue on it? Well I suppose that I did love it until I loved it no more that it became painful to me or un-enjoyable, and that is why I am not feeling pain now, but I know I can experience it if I recreate it again. But because now I really do know that I have not forgotten my previous pains, I do know what I have experienced and what I am feeling, and I also I do know how to deal with my feelings and now I do not choose to re-experience my pains of feelings as I did before.

I do remember!
Yes you love everything. Since having loved everything, you chose your love experience very carefully as so not to re-member your last pains or your sufferings as you would call them. Some chose to work for others, while some chose to work for themselves, while others chose the streets for themselves, while others chose to go to school, while others chose to do Nothing at all, and most importantly they all chose what they love and that is, they made their choices very carefully to can experience any best feeling of love from imagination of memory that they are and as they have thought themselves sharing that same thought at that moment of instant with someone who has made a choice. I know you have a question, but also know that you have the answer, which is the best part about these notes. You would ask yourself but does a child choose to be born in suffering, does it decide so willingly to be birthed into horrible situations and conditions, events or circumstances? And indeed you are all good in asking yourself these questions so that you may not ask them again.
I am actually a bit shocked to can realize that I am asking about something I know already. I know the answer because I have written it a few pages up, and that is on page 11. But to imagine myself to have forgotten is even more shocking than the realization itself. And this is all on few pages back up.

Good, all good.
You do remember.
Yes I do remember.
So then, after realizing that you can achieve a lot in one day, you chose your quest. So now that you know that a day is made of day of day and night of day. Try to imagine this then, even though you are not going to try to imagine it but actually imagine it now, you will find, discover and realize and most importantly remember that you can sleep at any given time of the day, and since you know this , why don't you not try imagining this?: If you could.

• Sleep and fall into sleep dream state from anytime you do not see or observe sunlight (8pm summer time and 7pm winter time) for twelve hours.

- Wake instantly on sunrise just after night of day (5am summer time and 6am winter time) after twelve hours.
- In doing this you will need tools that which you call timers. It can be anything you choose it to be. Do so until you do not need them anymore
- If it so happens that you wake up during night before sunrise, keep on sleeping.
- After you get used to it, try doing what you do in the night during the day, and what you do during the day in the night. In other words, try swapping you day activities to night and night activities to day.
- If you should feel that you do not want to swap, then well it is, because it is the same thing.

Remember that you do not have to do this, and that it is not a must to perform the above mentioned. This is not a practice, we are only remembering and realizing our imagination from our memory here.

So what we are accomplishing here is to make realize and make you even more aware of your beautiful created dreams. Yes all dreams are beautiful, all of them and you are beautiful too my loving, yes indeed you are. Most of you, especially you my loving son have forgotten your dreams. I know this and you know this as well. It is only of this current year you started having to remember some of your dreams, even though not most but at the least a few. You even went to a point of writing them down at some moment of time and did not keep up with it because of your daily work, church, school and going out partying and clubbing activities. You did not understand and or remember your dreams, especially your own dreams. How can you help someone achieve their own dreams when you are not having to create, understand and achieve and live your own? You got tired of not living your dream, but since because you had forgotten what your dreams are, you kept on with your daily loving struggle activities. At some time you revisited your dreams just by sharing them to some people you have regarded very close or most frequently spent time with.

But now Thato you are realizing your dream. You are waking up. And I mean exactly that. You are waking up. Now for many people including you, do not know what is to be awake, and being awake is to simply sleep and remember your most precious, and only your very own most precious loving dream you have always wanted to do and be, only that and Nothing else but that. And here comes the biggest question.

Why am I still struggling?

And the answer as always is that you have it in with you. You are waking up from and into something you do not like. Since you do not like your dreams, you have thus woken up back into your own little unlike world and understandable nightmare of doing something that you do not love, and this is the sad side you call reality because you think that you are not dreaming it. And because you think you are not dreaming it, how can it be? And after all you do not understand your dreams, how can you wake up into that which you do not understand? So be it then that you wake up to your own reality that you understand. So yes, this is the reason why you wake up from a nightmare of a dream to a nightmare dream of reality that you have chosen to label life. You wake up from a dream because you are not enjoying it, and thus come back to your sad little reality of dreams called reality. And whenever you have a very good dream, you forget how to go back into it, and you forget to do it on the realistic side as well.

Now that you know you can sleep dream in the day of a day and night of a day or night of a day and day of a day, you should know this.

You should know that you will never stop dreaming, you will never stop using your imagination because you are dreaming all the time and every day of the day and every night of day. It is all one thing, just as you are one thing. It appears to present itself as two because you are doing two different things. If you were doing what you preciously and most dearly love in your dreams, you will, would and can bring your dreams with you anywhere you choose. So then, choose to bring your dreams, bring your most dearly closely loved precious dreams with you to this side called reality. All of this can be done, Nothing cannot not be done!

So as you have created the day into night of day and day of day.

And so have you done the same with dreams. You made an observation that you are dreaming all the time, and in your dreams you realized and became aware of loved and strongly held dreams. And this was and is all good. These loved and strongly dearly held dream you thus called them reality. They are a reality because you realized that, that which you love

20

and strongly hold, you thus and strongly willingly create, and that is why you realize what you create. And so it was as it should be that you created your reality in your own dream. You took a whole dream and split it into two dreams, one is just simply dreams, and the other is reality of dreams. This is what is meant by make your dreams a reality. But can you really make your reality a dream? No... no... no, you argue it with yourself that, that which is real cannot be a dream, but then again how can I, and why should I make my dreams a reality if my reality is not my dream?
But all of this does not make sense.
It does not make sense because you think you are not dreaming, and you are looking at it from one perspective of realized dream which again you call reality. What should be done is that it should be looked at as one whole full packaged dream of imaginative memory. You can walk to a person at this instant and tell them that, you are not enjoying your dream. He or she will ask you what is your dream or what do you not enjoy about or in your dream? You will explain your dream to the person and he or she will tell you to stop doing what you are doing and be what you truly dream to be, and stop doing what you think you are not dreaming to be. So then, stop... stop... stop it and see it. Just stop it for your sake, stop it. Stop it that which you do not like. Make it stop and only you can make it stop Thato my son.

Why do I keep on calling myself son?
It is because I am older than I think. Every clock turn makes you older. You are old now and you will be old then, and you will be old now again and then again. So yes Thato, you are your son because you know that you are older than you were and you will be older than you are. So then my son, be your own son. And now that you know that you are old, you can now take care of yourself. If you see yourself as old, the older you will take care of the younger you. This is one of the major reasons why you have parents minding what their children are doing. It is so because they know how they were and are when they are young, and also they know how they are in old age and that is why they will protect and love dearly their young, because they know how old they are and what they went through when they were young as you are now. And I mean exactly that. They know. Do you know that one day you will be old?
Yes I do. I do know that I will be old one day.

So if you see things from when you are old, you will definitely see things from when you were or are young. If young sees old why can't old see young? Surly old sees young. So then my child, so then my son see it all, see it all at once, see it all now, see it all now my father. And you shall see how you guide yourself from old to young, and not from young to old.

Wow... wow... wow. I did not know all of this, where is it all coming from? It is coming from the older you. It is because you know better when you are old.
So then I can call myself son and I can also call myself father?
Yes indeed you can, yes you can my son.
I love you father.
And I love you son.
Wow you love yourself hey!
And you love yourself too hey!
Oh indeed I love me and you love me, and I even love myself and we both love each other.
Okay father, now I think I am starting to understand it.
Yes my son you have been remembering yourself and you will get there because I am here, and I know you than I know me, and you know me than you know you. I know this because I have been there. Oh and yes you will know me.
Lol... wow that is just so funny.
Trust me I have been laughing at you the whole time, and I mean I have been laughing at myself the whole time because I can see it all from here, which is all so funny.

Your greatest wish is for you to stop suffering and struggling.
Well I know work is not suffering and that it is a great struggle to can keep up with. I also know that school is not suffering and that it is a great struggle to can keep up with. And I also know that doing Nothing is not suffering, and that it is a great struggle to can keep up with.
So then do be aware that whatever you struggle for, you shall suffer for. And also do be aware that struggle is suffering and suffering is struggle and they are both just that. You struggle suffering and you are suffering struggle and they are both Nothing at all, all together. If you do not choose any of them, Nothing will happen to you because you have chosen

none of them. You will have chosen not to struggle suffer or not to suffer struggle and not to struggle suffer and suffer struggle, and in the end you will be all right. I mean look at me, I am talking to you now because I am all right, and that is because everything I have done is all right, it is all okay ma G. you are okay now my son.

Okay father Thato, thank you for explaining all this to me.

Thank you son Thato for listening to all of this that I am sharing with you now. Now let us move to your next grand question.

Lol, yes… yes you know that it is grand because I know right?

Yes I do know it because you know it. You gave me the answer hence I am giving it back to you, I am in fact giving back to myself.

Okay then, my grand question is how am I born or how did I create myself or how was I created? Why take the process of developing to being, and not just be what I have always known myself to be. Why not just be where you are now, why go through all of this, is it all necessary? Why was I once a baby, child, youth then an adult?

How did I get here and why did I choose here, why this place?

Why… why… why… why?

Wow now that is a grand question indeed. I will try with all my level best not keep or make all of this scientific. Okay first let us freshen up your memory.

Cool.

First there is one thing that you know, and what you know you were and are thus told in school. You are and were told in biology or life science class of how a baby is born or came to being. I am not going to go too deep into scientific or biological explanation and wasting time on what is already written and explained, but we will touch on a few here, we will keep it simple and basic. What you were told is that it takes two people to can create or make a child, and just not any two people, they have to be female and male or male and female, and that it has to be opposite sex. You were then told that once you have two opposite sex, they had or have to intimately interact through intercourse penetration with each other. After that, you have the sperms going into the uterus and travelling through the fallopian tube to meet the egg. You were also told that the egg is from the woman's ovary which is sucked into the fallopian tube to meet up with the sperm and they both join and exchange information of both persons which is the male and female or female and male. Then the process of an embryo forms and then slowly changes or develops into a human baby. This is what you were taught. And now apart from what you were taught in school, you know that it only takes male and female to make a child, this is your observation, and you do not need to be taught this.

Now I am going to tell you something you have forgotten. I am going to remind to you something you know. Before knowing yourself to be in this form, you were a thought and an imagination and you still are. You Thato my good friend are a man or male and a woman or female. Oh do not worry I will explain it all to you. First, let us start with the woman side of you.
Okay.

Your mother knew that one day she would give birth to a child, she knew of only that one day, and that one day is not specific or was specified. This means that it could be and has been any random day as long as it is that one day, and it also means that she always had you as a thought. A woman also knows that most men would love for their first born child to be a boy or a son, thus a thought and imagination is and was created for a son. So there you have it, a thought of imagination of a son has been created, and that very same thought of imagination was kept very close and dearly, it was recognized, appreciated and loved as it is now. So Thato my son, you as a thought spent a lot of time with your mother before you even took the formation of being what you are now. Everywhere she went, everything that she did you were there as a created thought of imagination with her in her thoughts, and you experienced what and who she was and is as a woman. Your mother also knew that whatever she was doing was all for that thought of imagination to can experience good life. Yes your mother wished and wanted you to have and experience good life, no parent does not wish so. And there you have it. You know what a woman is and you have been in the thoughts of imagination of a woman, which in this case is your mother.

The same thing can be said about you being a man. Most men wish for their first born to be a son or boy. Your Father always knew that one day he would give birth to a son or boy, although his first born was a girl from a different woman, he always kept a thought of imagination of having a son very close and dearly, and that is why you are a son born as first from your mother's side. And so as it was and is with your mother. You went everywhere and did everything with your father as a thought of imagination. Your father also knew that whatever everything that he is doing is all for you so that you can have it better than he did. All fathers and daddies wish the best for their children, and or but it is not in most cases recognized, it is not recognized because you do not understand what a shared thought is... but for now this is how you are both a male and a female. You are both through created thought of imagination from both your mother and father. They thought about you first even before they met each other and you in this form.

Then finally your mother and father came together as a couple to know their different interests, experiences and to share their sex physically by tasting, touching, informing, feeling and sexually intercourse each other. Now remember that even though they both may not realize at that moment that their strong held thought is present with them, and that is to say you were there with them Thato my Son, you saw and experienced yourself into creation, they were actually creating it and you. Also re-member that no specific day or date was set but only that one day, only that one precious day, they both knew they would have a son or a boy one day, and that is why you are precious, you are because you were born on a precious day of now. And on that day thus you were created and formed into being from a thought of imagination to being a physical being of imagination. So yes, you are a male now and you know how it is like to be a woman because you spent a thought time as a woman. You are not half a woman or half a man, you are a full woman and a full man. Hence you can act the role of a woman if you want or choose to.

Okay I hear you, but I still have a question.
I know and I still have the answer. Lol.
If I was first a thought of imagination, where was I all the time as a thought then?

Oh my... I love your question.
Like I said before, you were with your mother and father in their thoughts of imagination. But I do understand what you are asking. You want to know what you did meanwhile as a thought right?
Yes I do.
Okay then son or father, know this.
A thought of imagination is a living being. So far you know that you are a being and you call yourself human being instead of physical thought human being. The most important word here is physical. A thought also knows that it is a being, in other words it is imagination perceiving thought to being. So now we know a thought is a being, we can call it physical thought being and not physical being. So now you know all of this, I can now answer your question. And your question is what is it that you were doing while being a thought? The answer is so simple you will even laugh at it. You were doing what you are doing now and then and you are still doing it now. You were everywhere as a thought being thought itself to be. Since thoughts of imagination can be anywhere, you were everywhere you imagined yourself as a thought to be. All the places you have been to, all the things that you have done, and all the things you have thought to have done, you did them as a thought already. And now you are here, typing, reading, holding a book and asking me, and not forgetting that I am you about yourself of how you got to this point, and how you became to be. This is you expressing thought as were once and will always be. You my friend are a living physical thought parallel and in lineage to thought being. So yes thoughts are alive, thoughts are good and thoughts are very treasurers as they are your creative imagination of memory.

Thank you so much for explaining in such an understandable manner.
Thank you for the knowledge you have given and left for me.
Thank you for being Thato the father you are now.
And thank me for being Thato the son I am now.
Oh life, how so meaningful and meaningless you are.
You are the beginning and the end that goes back to the beginning.
I love my life and I love my thoughts of imaginative memory that which I am now.

I seek not to forget and forsake myself in the moment of my existing memory.

Oh my sweet memory I love you for you have reminded and remembered me.

All is well and what is well is all. Thank you all well. Thank you mother, thank you father, thank you daughter and thank you son.

Oh... I just needed to get that out of my chest.

Ahhhhhhgggggrr... it's all good ma G.

Okay I think get the whole birth and creation of myself so far.

So far! You mean there is actually more than what I have just told you now?

Yes I do think there is more, but so far I am satisfied of how I came to physical existence.

Ah... point of correction, you are a thought physical being.

Okay before you continue and tell me a whole lot of stuff here, I would like to ask something. Why do I not like or enjoy being alone? I mean, why do I get paranoid and irritated when I am alone in my own personal space? Even when I think that I am enjoying my me time, it is just only for a while, and after I just want to go see people, I just want to so desperately leave my room or house and see what is out there, I crave to see how people are doing and what they are being. Why do I have to feel that way? Can I not just be alone and enjoy myself?

Man you and your questions. I love them though. Very well then, let's get to it. Your question is the very big, and the main grand reason why you are here. You are here because you want and have chosen to experience yourself with others like you.

You wait a minute here. You told me that I am a created thought being from my parents and that whatever it is that I am doing now I have already thought myself to have done. And now you are telling me that I came here to experience myself with others, and not just any other but others like me. So what exactly are you saying hey? Are you trying to confuse me or what?

Hhhhhhmmm.... Why would I confuse myself? Would you at least let me finish, please let me finish and you will see that what you have asked now the answer will be given to. See, there is no limitation to imagination, the only limit is the limit that the imagination gives itself by thought. You now know that you are a thought of imaginative memory and you have thought yourself to be anywhere and everywhere you have been because you remembered. Now then, the reason why you feel that you should be with people is that there is actually and literally Nothing to do!!

Yes, there is Nothing to do. When you are all alone there is no experience, the only experience you will have and get is yourself. And yes indeed you are experiencing yourself inevitably each moment. You and most of many of you consider words to be real, and after words you consider action which is movement to be real. If no word is spoken it is not real to you, and if no action is taken or made, and that is to say if no movement is made it is also not real to you. And we know that words can be voiced and heard, and we also know that action or movement can be seen and observed... but wait a minute what about thought? Is thought not real, oh my... you never thought of that did you? You and most of many of you consider thought not to be real, but if thought is not real, then that means that everything I have done and everywhere I have been is not real because everything that is now was first thought to be. So now change your thoughts about your thoughts and make thoughts first reality. Nothing can ever come to existence without being thought of, everything that you now see and have heard was first thought to be, and every thought that was and is ever thought to be is first imagined, and imagination is memory of you. So yes my son make thoughts real because that's just what they are, they are real.

Here, let us look at something funny.

When someone walks into a room or a house and finds you or any other person talking alone or as you would put it, "talking to themselves"... they would ask, "why are you talking to yourself?... are you crazy?!" And if you tell them that, "I am just voicing out my thoughts", they will really give you that insane crazy look.

But and funny enough, when that very same person walks into a room or a house and finds you or someone cleaning, whether it is washing dishes, scrubbing the walls or just sweeping the floor, they would greet you with a smile or do whatever they came to do because they can see that you are cleaning or doing something, they can see action or movement of thought. He or she will not ask why you are cleaning by yourself, or are you crazy?! Should he or she curiously ask why you are cleaning and you

28

simply respond by saying that you are just acting or moving your thoughts, oh... they would really be confused and would give you that insane crazy look. And in truth that is exactly what all of you have been doing, that is what you have been doing. You have been voicing out your thoughts and you have been acting or moving your thoughts physically. So all of you, all of you right now are one big thought, you can be a thought thinking itself to be, or a thought voicing itself or acting or moving itself to being. You are all thinking. You are a thought moving, voicing and thinking all together in different rhythms.

Now let's get to your answer.
You are here to experience yourself with others. When you are all alone, you get bored because you realize that there is Nothing to do accept for being who you are, and who you are is really Nothing at all. So now since you knew that there is Nothing to do, you then decided to do what you are not doing, and what you are not doing is Nothing at all, hence you leave your room and go see and experience the Nothingness of others, yes Nothingness of others. You leave your room or house to share the Nothingness of others.

Let me remind you.
When a person, and that can be your mother, son, brother, father, sister, cousin or any other relative and most specially you is alone in a room or space of a house or an isolated outdoor environment, there are a lot of things one can do. You could for instance:
Listen and dance to your favorite music.
Cook or prepare a meal that you love the most.
Read a book to inform yourself and gain knowledge of wisdom.
Watch a movie, series or soapy or a documentary.
Relax in a nice cold or warm bath or take good old new shower.
Swim in a river or be at the beach alone in no one's presence but yours.
Take a nice nap.
Rub and massage yourself smoothly and gently.
Enjoy a nice cold drink of any sort of your choice.
Have good old smoke while thinking and reflecting back.
Please and pleasure yourself in a stimulating and interesting arousing way by touching and feeling yourself and playing with your genital, yes

stimulate yourself because no one knows you better than you do, you know your good spots better.

Well sadly enough, I hate to say it, but these are the most frequent human activities. This is what people do, this is what they get up to, and this is what people enjoy doing the most. The only one thing that troubles them which in turn creates a problem is that they know that they are doing all of these things, and in their knowing they get bored doing them alone. Oh yes it is quiet boring all alone, and that is why you find people who will rather go to a church, school, pub or club and have a great drinking time, great music time and a great dancing or learning time with others rather than alone. People do not like to sit in the house and think all day all alone, they rather go and share their thoughts that they are thinking now in their alone space with someone. People do not like to cook and enjoy their food alone every day to themselves all the time, they rather invite someone or you over and share with you. People do not want to talk to themselves all day every day all the time, they rather come to your house and tell you what their future plans are and what they plan to do, which is what they have thought of in their boredom and alone space. People do not like to please, arouse and stimulate themselves, they rather go and give someone else the pleasure they have been giving themselves.

Oh yes there really is Nothing to do!
And there is so much to do in Nothingness.
You see, when you start to move from Nothing to something, that is when limitation is met. Limitation is met because you have set yourself to a particular course or task, hence then it is labeled something. You embark on a course to a particular thing which in turn you have labeled it anything that comes from Nothing. Yes my son there is Nothing to do and everything to be and do in Nothing. If you have Nothing to do, you will not be particular in doing anything. So as you have asked me why you mostly feel to leave your room or your own alone space, that is my answer to you. There is Nothing to do. All of you are doing Nothing now at this moment of this instant and instance, you do not see it because you are sharing and experiencing your boredom with others. This is a shared thought of choice. Let me, the older you ask a question. What would you do if you had all the money you thought you could ever have?
Okay, first thing on my mind is that I will travel.

Okay, good.

Why would you need, feel, like or love to travel?

I would like to travel because, I would love to see the world and meet different people, I would like to enjoy myself with other people, I would like to give and receive pleasure in its all forms from and to other people.

Wow, now that is a fair answer.

All is good and good is all, but do you really think that you need to travel to can experience all that you have mentioned above?

Mmmhhh…. That is a tricky one.

Okay, let me help you get closer to it. Which places would you like to travel to and why?

I would like to go to space and observe my planet earth, go to New York City, London, Paris, central and north Africa, Egypt, Scotland, Brazil, Japan and Australia.

Wow that is plentiful and handful of travelling hey! But you still have not answered me why? What is there to see there?

Okay I see what you mean. Well I want to see planets, people, different mega cities and beaches and eat different food, experience different cultures and tribes. I want to do things I have never done before.

Okay, and what is it exactly that you have never done before?

Well there are lots of things. I would like to do deep blue diving, sky diving, paragliding, ride an elephant, observe the earth from out in space, see big falls, be with different people man, and so on and on and on.

I tell you this, I have done all of those things.

You have?

Yes I have, I have because you have thought yourself to have been there in your thought of imaginative memory. But for now I understand your understanding, and that is why we will talk about this later.

Okay.

Hhhhhhmmm…… So tell me, you would travel all the way only to experience all of those things?

Yes, I mean if having all the money for that, why not experience them and all of it?

Well, fair enough…. Now let me tell you this. You now stay in Cape Town of South Africa of the continent Africa of the Plane Earth, have you ever marveled how beautiful this city is? Have you ever given yourself a moment to realize how many plentiful and handful of beaches you have here? Have you seen the real beauty of Table Mountain, have you really been to Cape Town, and I mean like really in to the heart of Cape Town, and if you have, have you really appreciated it, have you thanked it for its magnificence and beauty?

I tell you this, each and every single continent has its beautiful beaches, each and every single continent has a beautiful people, each continent has big beautiful small cities and also provided that there are casinos, clubs, bars, taverns, hotels, restaurants, supermarkets, mini-local shops, brothels, woman, men, prostitutes, food of any sort, drinks of any sort, mountains, snow or ice, dry land, forests, animals and plants. All of this and these has and have been placed perfectly fairly. You do not need or have to sail the ocean or fly over it to the next or opposite land just to experience it differently. Land here is the same as there, and sea water or ocean here is the same as there, in fact they are one thing. People here are the same as there, they all have emotions, and you know all their emotions because you have experienced them. Same features that you find on a woman here you will find on a woman there, and the same features that you find on a man here you will find on a man there. It is all the same, it is all one thing and it is all connected and multiplying.

So then, yes as it should be, this is why you are here, this is why you chose this place and this is why... why... why?.... You are here to experience yourself with others like you through thought of imaginative memory, and you are all alike. That is why you said that you would travel if you had money. You would do so because you choose to experience what you have now differently the same as you have it now. You would do that because you are bored. There is Nothing that you can do overseas or there that you cannot do here, and there is Nothing that you could not have done here but could have done overseas or there. Whatever you can do here, you can do it there. Oh no do not get me wrong here, there is Nothing wrong with travelling and there is Nothing right with travelling, I am just making an awareness and realization of what extreme you can put yourself into.

Wait a second here, what do you mean by extreme?

Oh... well I simply mean that you can work yourself off for one, two, three ten or even more years acquiring money for just simple experiences and adventures. Experiences and adventures that you can have now where you are, right here in Cape Town, right here in South Africa, right here in Africa and finally I can say right here on planet Earth because it is one thing happening at this moment. It is all the same. I already know how you would feel, but I want you to say it and tell it to me. Tell me one thing here... how would you feel if you would be or were at the Eiffel Tower in Paris or at the statue of Liberty in the United States?

Wow, now it would feel great, I would feel good to be there, I would shout yeah, hell yeah I am here... from the top of the tower, I would take pictures to remind myself that I was there. It would be great to be there. I can just imagine myself having a beautiful view of Paris or New York and its people. Oh how nice it would be just to be there, just a thought of it fills me with joy and excitement already. Wow it would really be good to be there.

Yes... yes... and yes, that is exactly how you would feel if you were and are there. You have just given yourself the feeling of being in Paris at the Eiffe Tower or at Liberty Island in New York on the statue of Liberty, and that is exactly how you would and will feel when you are there now. The joy, happiness, feel good feeling and full of smiles and thoughts of telling everybody back at home of how it is to be there and how it feels. That is the whole point of being there. There is Nothing else but that. You would be there just to give yourself the feeling that you have just explained and experienced now.

Wow really?

Yes!

So now that you know the feeling and what you will experience when you are there, do you still really think that you should go there just to have the same feeling that you have just experienced now? Do you really think it is necessary? Surly not. I tell you this, this is exactly what people have made necessary, this is what you would make necessary and this is what you would work for so hard and for so many long years just to give yourself the feel good experience. This is what you would suffer for, and this is what people are suffering for. And also this is the measure of extreme you would put yourself into and or die for.

I tell you this.

You do not want to suffer but you like the things suffering can bring you. Let me tell you what I mean by this. You my son and many of you do not like or love going to work, especially if it is the kind of work that you never set yourself out for or dreamt of. It can be any kind and type of work, and it can pay lots or the minimum least of money, you would still not like it. But hey, there are things which you like about this kind of suffering, there are things of which you think and believe that they are of benefit to you and those close to you. Let us see what these things are, let us have a close observation and detail these things out for the sake of me and you and many of you and me. The first reason why you have chosen to work is the knowing thought that you need money, but this is not your main thought, your main thought is to be there where you want to be, and that is to say to be and live your dream. And where you want to be is where you are right now, and you will find a way to get to your dream until you get to it where you are right now. You were told that you need money. You were trained and tamed and brought up with the need for money, and you have kept the words and deeds of money since ever then. Thus this has become your thought, thus this has become your knowledge. Since you think, know and believe that you need money, you then saw, observed and realized that having acquired money can get you to places, it can get you things, and it can even get you people.

Oh…. Wow, how beautiful money is, and how good it feels to have money you told yourself. But funny enough you always knew that you did not need it, and you knew its troubles and what conditions and states it can leave a home in. You my son saw and observed the need and distractions of money, you saw the beauty and the beast of money at an early age. So you then decided to work, you thought of doing something that could help you acquire money, and also because you were bored and had Nothing to do. You thought of what to do to acquire money. You decided to work, it did not matter to you then, because you knew that you did not have any experience of sort concerning work, so you told yourself whatever comes will do for you. The thought of staying at home as a teenager and doing Nothing just did not work for you. You could not stand the thought of dependency, you wanted independency from anyone. You wanted to ease off things for your mother, you wanted to ease off things for your father, and you wanted what was better for you. You wanted what makes you happy, and what made you happy was and is independency from anybody and or anything.

Now let's see what money can acquire for you.
Money can acquire you food easily and quickly, and if you have a bit more it can get you the food that you would specifically like, and if you have a bit more than more, it can acquire more and any kind of food that you desire to have. So then, ask yourself what kind of food are you? Do you eat anything or any simple food, and what is simple food anyway? Do you choose your food or are you very particular? And yes this is one of many that money can have to you.
Money can acquire you with clothes easily and quickly, and if you have a bit more, it can get you the clothes that you specifically like, and if you have a bit more than more, it can acquire more and any kind of clothes that you desire to have, I am talking about designer labels and expensive clothes and brands. So then, ask yourself what clothes are you? Do you wear any simple clothes, and what are simple clothes anyway? Do you choose your clothes or are you very particular of what you wear? And yes this is one of many that money can have to you.
You are already born in a shelter, the earth is your prime shelter hence you take soil, plants, water and rocks to build houses from it. You do not need money for this, but in this case; Money can acquire you with a house very easily and quickly, and if you have a bit more, it can get you the house that you specifically like, and if you have a bit more than more, it can acquire more and any kind of houses you desire to have, I am talking about big houses, flats of apartments and mansions here. So then ask yourself what kind of house are you? Do you live in any simple house, and what is a simple house anyway? Do you choose your house or are you very particular in what kind of a house you live or stay in? And yes this is one of many that money can have to you.
Money can acquire you a woman easily and quickly, and if you have a bit more, it can get you a woman that you specifically like, and if you have a bit more than more, it can acquire more and any kind of woman you desire to have, I am talking about what you consider really beautiful, pretty, hot and sexy woman here. So then ask yourself what kind of a woman are you? Do you do any simple woman, and what is a simple

woman anyway? Do you choose your woman or are you very particular with what kind of a woman you sexually engage or relate with? And yes this is one of many that money can have to you.

Money can acquire you a man easily and quickly, and if you have a bit more, it can get you a man that you specifically like, and if you have a bit more than more, it can acquire more and any kind of man you desire to have, I am talking about what you consider really beautiful, pretty, hot and sexy man here. So then ask yourself what kind of man are you? Do you do any simple man, and what is a simple man anyway? Do you do men at all, or do you choose your man or are you very particular with what kind of a man you sexually engage or relate with? And yes this is one of many that money can have to you.

Money can acquire you a car easily and quickly, and if you have a bit more, it can get you a car that you specifically like, and if you have a bit more than more, it can acquire more and many kinds of cars you desire to have, I am talking about your VW Polo, Ferrari, Lamborghini, Jeep, Mercedes and Range Rovers here. So then ask yourself what kind of a car are you? Do you drive any simple car, and what is a simple car anyway? Do you choose your cars or are you very particular with what kind of a car you drive? And yes this is one of many that money can have to you. From here there onwards what follows is extra, what follows is more and more plentiful and handful extra.

I have mentioned above top major reasons why you work and put yourself to such extremes. I have mentioned the things and benefits suffering can bring to you. You actually get killed for these things, you kill for these things, you get hurt for these things, you cheat for these things, you lie for these things, you steal for these things... oh my... you are actually all of these things. Yes my son, you suffer and struggle for these things and all of you actually struggle and suffer for these things. But never the less, this is what you enjoy, you do not enjoy the struggle and suffering process but no...no....no, you enjoy what that struggle and suffering brings and has to offer to you. You love it my man... so as long as you love it, why make it stop, why change what is so good and sweet, bitter at the same time and tinkles while filling you with confusion and despair?

Oh how good is my struggle, how nice is my own created suffering and its pleasures. Oh how good are the pains of my hunger, I am weary but in all of it still relentless. I love you life, you have had me to live, and you are showing me the way towards me. I choose not to forget my existence, help me live and be life. Oh… oh help me life, hold me and tell me that you love me, tell me that you will never let me go, be with me forever, let me touch you and you touch me. I want to be married to you, I want to be alive as you life. Oh life you are eternal, you are forever more, and you are the beginning and the end that is at the beginning. Let me be you, let you be me, oh let us be one, and let us be together.

Lol… wow.
Wow Thato it sounds like you are in love there hey?
Well what if I am in love so what?
Yes indeed so what if you are in love? And what are you in love with or who are you in love with?
Why are you asking me a question that you already know?
Oh well I just want you to say it, please… please me by saying it.
Okay… do not beg please. I am in love with life. Oh I love my life and I love it.
Mmmmm….. I can see that, and it's good to see you smiling and feeling all like this.
Thanks man.
Oh no thank you man.

You have remembered.
So yes I tell you this. Everything that you have experienced, you have thus experienced and created out of boredom. You are suffering because you do not want and choose to be alone, you are sad and unhappy because you do not want and choose to be alone, you get hurt because you do not want and choose to be alone, you thus and always will as long as you are with others experience disappointment because you do not choose to be alone. Come closer, let us talk about it. Who is making you sad? Who is making you cry? Who is making you to be angry? Who is making you unhappy and grumpy? Who is making you beg? Who is causing you pain and grieve and finally we can say who is causing you to love? I tell you this, you and many of you are causing these feelings and pains to yourselves. By making a choice to spend at any moment with anybody is always crucial, you are guaranteed to have and experience any emotion

with them or around them. Your mother has once made you upset and angry, but you know what? She has once in a moment of time as well made you very happy and full of joy. So do you see how even our loved ones can hurt and make us happy? When I say us, I mean me and you Thato my son. Now you have asked me why you leave your alone space and be with someone, these are the reasons and boredom is one of them. And why are you bored? It is because there is Nothing to do around here except for being who you are. And who you are is Nothing at all.

Remember this!
Yes you have remembered.
There are many ways of escaping boredom and being hurt with or around others. And the funny part is that you have been very little doing so, and you can do it more than just very little, you can do it greater. You have always told yourself that you love everybody equally no matter what status, race, colour, nationality gender or sex, this my son you have kept it a little while with you and it has now become you. It is what defines you as Thato.
Mmmmm…. Yes that is true, I do love everybody the same no matter what status, race, colour, nationality and gender or sex. I love them all as I love my mother, I love them all as I love me. Honestly this is what I feel, this is me and I would not change anything of it.
Yes my son, I know that, that is you. And you have been all good and good you have been all.
I love everybody, I mean I do not see any fault in them or anyone.
However there is that one thing I do not like of or about people. I do not like people's behaviors, their attitudes and how they hate and dislike each other….
Wait a minute here Thato, before you go any further, you said that you love everybody equally the same right?
Yes.
And you also said that you do not like people's behaviors and attitudes as well right?
Yes, I said exactly that.
Okay, let me remind you what you have forgotten. Remember that I told you that you are a living thought, and that is to say you are a thought and

everything that you do, say or act out comes from your thoughts of imagination of memory that you are.

Ahhhhmmm... yes I do remember that.

So then, do observe and realize that someone's action of behavior and attitude is and comes from their thoughts, it is how they have conceptualized things, and it is who they are at that moment of instant. So when you say that you love them, however you hate their behaviors and attitudes you are actually saying that you hate them... isn't it funny?

Wow... thank you for making me realize all of this... oh thank you so much

Ahhhh... no worries about a thing coz every little thing is going to be alright just like Bob Marley said.

Hahahahahah... lol, very funny hey!

And that is the next topic here.

What, Bob Marley?

Sshhhh..... Take it easy brother I am getting there, let me take a breather for bit. And yes, I am not trying to run away from explaining how to escape boredom, I will and I cannot because we have been talking about one thing here, so do not worry we will get back to what I was saying okay.

Okay cool.

You see Thato my son, you are a memory and as you are a memory, you love to record yourself as a memory, and that is what you have been doing, that is what most if not many of you have been doing. You have and all of you everywhere have recorded a memory as a memory somewhere somehow. Do not get confused yet, I am still explaining how this is all so.

Okay.

Have you ever taken a picture of yourself?

Ahhhh... man do I even need to answer that?

No you do not, but if you do not I will answer it for you.

Why didn't you just answer it from the start then, why didn't you just say it without asking me the obvious?

Well I wanted to get you engaged in this conversation. You know it is quite boring when you are talking to yourself, I might start to think that I am crazy, ooohhh... people might just think that I am crazy you know... lol... oh wait a minute you might just think that I am crazy.

Lol... I can see you are trying to be funny hey, you got jokes for universes. Fine let me answer your question then. Yes I have taken a picture of myself and of others.

Good, that wasn't so difficult now was it?

No it was not.

So now then listen to this, in one way or the other all of you have recorded themselves. There are many ways that you have done so, some of you have taken pictures of themselves, drew, sculptured or painted themselves. Some of you have written down notes of themselves on diary, note sheet, device or a book or just on one piece of paper. And some of you have taken videos of themselves, some of you have made music of themselves both voice and instruments, while others just chose to be a memory as they already are and know themselves to be. Yes you love to record and freeze memory of you in a moment instant of time of memory. You want to touch, feel, hear and see yourself as memory that you already are, this is what all of you are doing. You may be doing it consciously or unaware, but this is what you all as whole are doing my son, you are recording yourselves and your existence. No matter what form of record you choose to use, it is beautiful and it defines and expresses who you are my son. This is one of the main grand major reasons why selfies have become a trend. They have become a trend because you love to record yourself as a memory.

In your moment of time now, the most frequent form of record is music. Music is loved by many, music is used by many of you to express yourselves, and music is also understood by many. Every single song or track of music that has or is released is beautiful and it is good. And not only is it beautiful and good it is meaningful to you and the artist as well.

You have remembered!

I tell you this, music is your grand communicator of your now time. If you could listen to every single track or song that is playing on radio, home record, church, clubs, small devices or internet carefully, you would be very surprised at what it has to offer you, it is actually expressing your feelings and who you are. Yes I know sometimes you say that, but the beat of instruments is not so good of that one particular song. But did you really listen and hear to what it said? Or even vice versa, it may have what you consider as bad lyrical contents, but did you really hear how good the instruments were? And finally it may have what you consider as good instruments and tune and have good lyrics and you would still say, "nahhhh... that is not my genre, I do not like that song." But did you really feel and hear what it had to offer you? In your music you talk about how very lustful you are and what you would do to a girl or a boy if he or she showed you this and did that. Oh how much it would please you to get and do all of that and this.... and guess what? This is what you love and listen to, and this is what you dance to in clubs and in your rooms or homes.

In your music you talk about how angry you are and how much pain you feel or have felt, and how you would kill someone if they did this or that, oh how you would really hurt someone... and guess what? This is what you love and listen to, this is what you dance to in clubs and in your rooms or homes. You say that it represents who you are. In your music you talk about how much you love people or that one special particular person, oh how much you miss them, oh how you wish they were here with you. How special and how much they mean to you, oh how much you really love.... and guess what? This is what you love and listen to, this is what you dance to in clubs and in your rooms or homes, this is what you say, it defines you as who you are. In your music you talk about your Creator, His Son, Prophet, Teacher, the Supreme and how much you adore and worship thee, oh how much you will defend and kill for thee. Oh how much you need thee, for you feel lost without thee... and guess what? This is what you dance to in clubs and at places of worship, this is what you listen to in your rooms and homes, and this is what you praise at places of worship my son.

You have remembered.
Yes, I do remember.
So can you now see how you talk and communicate to each other all the time and every moment? This is what you have chosen to be your grandest communicator and expresser, this tool called music is who you are. Every single track that is and has been released represents and describes how a certain particular artist was or is feeling at a particular moment of instant of now time. It may be crap, sad, scary, lonely, happy, joyful, blissful or lustful, in the end it is who they are and how they feel at this or that moment. And if you like it, then you feel that person. You

know what? He or she is talking about you, oh you really are that person my son because you share the same feelings. And when you feel sad you know which song to listen to, you know which one to pick ma G, if not, it will find you and you will relate to it. It will talk to you and you will feel better afterwards, because you know that you are not the only one, you are not alone, it is not only you experiencing these emotions my son. All of you are and I mean pieces of all of you everywhere my son.

Wow... Phheeww man, you can really talk hey!

And you really have the time to listen hey! I mean seriously have you really been listening to all of this? My man you are a listener, I like it, nice one man.

Sure ma G.

But I did not see things in this manner or way, and I did not know what you are telling me now.

Well I tell you this, you did know, you just have been ignorant and careless and thus you have forgotten. Had you really given yourself a moment to appreciate and listen, you would have realized it sooner and remembered. But you have been ignorant and careless, and it is all good and good is all my son.

Are you ever going to stop talking?

What? Are you tired of me already, do you want me to stop?

Well no I do not, you know what maybe I do, but I enjoy listening to you though man, you seem like cool wise guy. Lol.

Tell you what, if you are tired you can go and have a drink, snack, pee, walk, nap or go to school or work and you will find me here. I am not moving from this laptop, I will not move from this paper or book that you are holding now in your hand, and I will not move from this device as well. When you come back you will find me here on this bed, table, chair, train, car or in your hands reading out my thoughts and talking to you, you will find me here reading these notes to you my son, to you my daughter. I mean think about it, you can go to the lavatory now and when you come back, whenever it may be, you will find me here, you will find yourself right here asking me questions and typing, and reading all that I am saying right here now. It is almost as if you never moved, but you did move, and it is almost as if you did move, but never moved, and it is exactly that, you moved and you never moved. Who can be the witness to that? Well I tell you this, you are your own witness, you know what you did and how you did it, just like you know what you did last summer, you know it because you have done it through thought of imagination of memory first. Well we are still talking about music here, so let us not get carried away okay, lol. We will get to this later.

Okay sure, I am listening please continue.

You have remembered.

Sorry... wait here a bit, why do you keep on saying that you have remembered or I have remembered?

Ahhh... Thato, I am saying that because it is what we are doing here. Me and you my son are remembering what we know already, or did you forget already?

Nope I did not.

Yes I know you did not my son, it is and was just your curiosity troubling your mind. Very well then, now listen. I wanted to show you how it all works, I want you to see how it is, how all of it is. Me and you are going to select a few tracks or songs, you will select them and write them down by names only here on these notes, on your notes. You will not write them in full but just the song tittle and the artist. It does not have to be a special specific kind of song because all songs are beautiful, all songs are great and all songs are meaningful. The one that you choose and the one that you do not choose are both special my son.

Wow okay, that sounds like fun, come let us do it.

Hey take it easy buddy okay.

Do not tell me what to do! Or would you like to try me?

Ahhhhhh... oooohh... I am really scared, and I am sorry buddy I do not resolve with or in violence man. I mean look, I cannot even touch you, I can only talk to you and if you do not want or choose not to listen, it is all good and good is all.

Who said anything about violence?

Take a wild guess who is talking here, lol.

I am just kidding man, please let us start.

Okay let us do it ma G.

Track number one!

Nasir Jones
N.Y STATE OF MIND
Wow, now this song here, is one of all many best songs I have ever listened to. The rapper flows in a poetic manner while relating to the place or streets that he grew in. One can say that he was touched and moved by what was happening in his surrounding environment.
Is this the way the song has communicated with you?
Yes. Nas is a great rapper.
Okay, move to the next one.

Bob Marley
REDEMPTION SONG
Bob Marley. Wow, now this song is so very touchy, emotional, and I would think spiritual as well. I think the artist or singer felt that a lot of people were and still are being controlled, and that they do not express themselves as they feel to be. I would say that, he thinks we are a hopeless generation hoping on liberty without understanding the true meaning of freedom.
Is this the way the song has communicated with you?
Well, yes, and it is a very powerful song. Bob is a legend.

Marlon Roudette
NEW AGE
Now with this song here, I would say or think that the singer or artist was feeling love at its greatest, whether by loss or gain, whichever comes first, he sure is over it.
Is this how you feel about the song?
Yes, and Marlon is good singer.

J Cole
APPARENTLY
This is also a nice song, and I just love it. Thank you J Cole for reminding us of our mothers.

Earth, Wind and Fire
FANTASY
Wow, I love this song so much. It also contributed some of the stuff I am writing about here on these notes. The song itself promises a world of possible things through my imagined world.
Do you believe of what they sing about?
Lol, yes. They are a good band.
Okay.

Imagination
JUST AN ILLUSION
Yah hey. They are explaining and just about saying what you have been telling me throughout these notes. I like the song, I suppose their message is that it is all in our heads hey.
And do you think and believe so?
Lol, I have to say yes again.
Good, then move to next one.

Madonna
LIVING FOR LOVE
The lady who never ages. I think Madonna, has been through a lot in her music career. On this song according to me, is that she has gotten to this point, and that there is nothing to do because she has reached the level she has always dreamt of, and now that she is there on that level, there is nowhere else to go but there on that level. And that is why she will live it for love.
Is this how you feel about the song?
Yep. This is what I feel and think.
Okay, next one.

Kanye West ft. Paul McCartney
ONLY ONE
Lol, God himself. I would say Kanye was feeling compassion, sadness, loneliness, holy and the realization of the world as it unfolded before him. Emotions are mixed in this song, but I do get the message though.
Did you really get the message?
Yes, and it is a good song.

One Republic
COUNTING STARS
Basically we are a generation that is told what to do and how to do it and what is right and or wrong, and we are tired of that. But we feel to do what we are told not to do. We just want to be loose, wild and free to can best experience ourselves. And these are the things that our youth dream about and wish for.
Do you like the song?
Heck yes!

Don Moen
THIS IS YOUR HOUSE
Mmmmhhh... What a great song. The all of Holy is invited into my house to claim and own it. I have let the all of Holy to do everything for me, while I sit back and watch things manifest and come to being effortlessly.
I see that you love it.
Yah, it moved me when I first heard it.

Taylor Swift
SHAKE IT OFF
Yeah, you go girl. I guess it is one of those obvious songs when one feels that they do not care of what the other next person says. You will always have people hating on you for no reason whatsoever, but it does not matter if you can just shake it off, and in fact you should shake it off and go on about your way.
Okay, next one.

Nicki Minaj
ANACONDA
Mmmmhhh... I do not know what to say about this one. Well, if you have a nice big round firm behind, then this song is for you. I would assume that Nicki did not care who was to like or not like the song. She knew that she had the money to put it out there, and so out there it was. And guess what? Some people just love it.
And do you like the song?

Lol, well I like the video with all the nice girls in it, but as for words and lyrical content… come on, I could have also sang that with my bad voice.

Balance of power
BALANC OF POWER
This to me is meaningful. It tells that there is always someone there to be your shoulder and balance when things get heavy for you. It is an extra mile a person is willing to take for the other next person.
Good. Move to the next song.

Guns N' Roses
NOVEMBER RAIN
Guns N' Roses. Yah, hey. This song according to me, is about understanding the love that is now. I think it delivers a message that we should understand that everything changes, even the love that is now. Just love what you have and that which is around you now and know that the experience is not forever but eternal.
Yes, that is why I chose it for you.
Ah, I see. Lol.
Next one please.

Brenda Fassie
MY BLACK PRESIDENT
The song that touched and moved many South Africans. Brenda felt the love and hate of the nation, she was moved by the people to stand as a voice for the coming release of Nelson Mandela for the people.
Yah hey, this country went through a lot. It went through a lot that it exploded into many different colours of the rainbow. And so as it is as it should be, just as it is all good and good is all.
While we are on this subject, this reminds me. My mother and father went through that struggle era. Does this mean that I also experienced what they went through as a though just as you have said?
Yes you did.
Okay, I do not want to go into it that much, so I will move to the next song.

Eminem
WHEN I'M GONE
My man Slim Shady. On this song, Eminem is engaged in his true dream as
a rapper, and at the same time he dreams of his dream hurting the ones
he loves the most, the ones he would kill for at any moment of time. I
would assume he was going through a rough time.
Do you like the song?
Yes I do. Eminem is a great rapper.

Gorillaz
CLINT EASTWOOD
Release yourselves from the mind that you are trapped in. I think this
group on this song saw and observed that life means nothing but you as a
person. They also, like many other of us feel that we are controlled, and in
it being so, it is all in our heads.
Do you like their music?
Lol, yes I do, I mean I liked this song when I was younger because of the
animated characters, so I was drawn to it then, but did not understand
the lyrical content.
Okay then, next song.

Queen
RADIO GA GA
The love for radio music. Queen felt that radio music is rapidly losing
touch and time, and they just wanted to remind people that radio is not
going anywhere and that it is here to stay.
Do you like queen?
Well not that much, but this is a catchy song, it makes you want to move
and rock to it, you know what I mean?
Yes I do son, yes I do.

Adele
MAKE YOU FEEL MY LOVE
Nothing to say. Here we are blessed with a universal voice I think. I think
all people would do what this song says for their loved ones. This is love
despair at its definition. We all have found ourselves having to love

someone so much that we promise to do great things for them just to make them feel and see how much we love them.

Would you personally do all great things for your loved one?

Yes I will and can.

Thank you, and now you are ready to receive.

I have received it and I thank you.

It has been a great pleasure.

And Adele is a great lovely singer.

Okay then, move to the next song.

Michael Jackson

EARTH SONG

I really do not know what to say about this one. Wow Michael is a universal legend. This song is about all the confusion going on in the world today. It is a concerned, loving, spiritual and an awaited promise song. I really do not know what to say about it, but Michael was feeling sad, worried and at the same time caring.

Yes my son, Michael is special just as you are, and you are all special, all of you are very special my daughter.

Thank you again for your kind words.

Okay, I think we are done here.

Yah, that is almost all enough not.

Wow, we could go on forever here. I mean there are a lot of plenty songs we could put on the above small list and they still would not be enough. And also I know that you feel and see that I left out some songs that you would have loved to see here on these notes, but man aren't they many! Wow, we could end up filling the entire notes with other peoples' songs hey.

Do you see how beautiful, meaningful, sexy, sad and joyful a song is?

I tell you this, if you remove the artists names from the songs above and combine the lyrics, you can make one song out of that and even write a book. You will realize that the songs or lyrics become one thing, oh indeed they are one.

So what you are telling me or revealing to me, is that all the songs from all the albums of one individual artist can be transformed into poetry, novel or a biography of that particular artist?

Yes indeed, it is who they are, and that is why they release an album. An album is a book, and that is why it is called a record, and a book is a record full of memories and stories of you and the way you have chosen to experience life according to your perception of thought and feeling. So when you buy a music album, know that you are buying a book with different instrumental tempo and adjustments of flow and pitch over voice of expressed feelings of that one particular person. So yah, they are telling their story on how they are feeling right now at this or that moment through their music, and you buy how they feel and express themselves, you run to the internet for new downloads, and you even fill up music stores for new arrivals and releases. They even sometimes lie about what they are to can be what they lied about in their songs. And yes I do know that somewhere in you, you are arguing that, but some songs are pathetic, somewhere in you, you have observed that I have chosen a specific selection of tracks or song that has a message, so you would tell yourself. Well I tell you this, even the most pathetic and meaningless song you can ever think of whether it is by beat, and instruments or lyrical or voice contents is good and meaningful.

Are you confused? Well do not be, I am here to give you solutions as I have dedicated myself to.

Now let me explain it to you. Sometimes of moment of instant of time in your life, you have reached a point where you feel that life is pointless, a time where you feel it is meaningless and inexpressible, a time when you are confused and feeling pathetic, a time where you feel pressured and a time where you feel stupid, and I mean very stupid. This you have encountered my son, this is you. So then I tell you this, that very song you so much think is pathetic, that very same song is pathetically meaningful my son. That one song you so much think is very sexually explicit and dirty, that very same song is sexually explicitly meaningful my son, you have intently performed sexually explicit meaningful behaviors and activities in and outside your room or house my son, and if it was or is meaningless, you still have done it. You have done it by thought and action of thought. That one song you so much think is stupid, that very same song is stupidly meaningful my father. I mean come to think of it, if you had to perform or sing that one moment of instant of time when you were or are feeling stupid, how would it sound? Mmmmm, lol…. Do not worry you do not have to say it, I am you and you are me and I know your thoughts. Yes that is right, you can laugh all you want but that is true, this is your truth.

So then do see. Do realize. And most important do remember that all songs are memorable, and all songs are meaningful, all songs are beautifully good! They are pieces of you, and they resemble you and that is what is. You take it or reject, it matters not because that's just you. And now look at this. This is where it gets funny because you will soon realize what you already know. All events that have ever happened or occurred are written down on paper or on digital documentation, wait… wait… wait, hold that question of thought, let me explain it to you so that you do not have to ask it. I see your thought, I see it because I am your biggest thought my son. You want to ask or tell me that, but not all events are recorded, not everything is recorded, I mean there is a lot that happens hourly, daily and monthly and so on everywhere, but not all of it is recorded. Yes I do know that, and the reason why not all hourly, daily and monthly events are not recorded is because they have already been recorded, they have already been written about… wait… wait, keep your thoughts of question, I am getting there. I mean take a look at this, all sort, manner and approach or trigger of what you call crime, have been written already. All possible crimes are known to you, and you even wrote down all possible causes to each crime, you have written psychological and philosophical books about crime and what motivates one to commit a criminal act and you have thus given solutions to crime itself the way you think is best suited. You see, it has already been written, that is why there is no need to re-write what you know over and over and finally over again. You have done the same with love, hate, anger and blah… blah… blah, you know man the rest of feelings.

So then before your question of thought came to you, all events that have ever occurred are written down. Even the most little and less regarded events have been written down, that is why you will find what you call silliest, pathetic and futile things in your magazines. A magazine can post a toe, hips and or a hair style of a particular celebrity and how he or she lives and what he or she drives or eats. It even posts married celebrity couple caught kissing and squeezing or cheating or shouting at each other in public sight as if it was a new thing or something is funny or wrong about it. But you know what? You still read magazines because they represent who you are, and who you are is recorded on in your memory as you are. And you are all just being silly Thato.

Man you are just full of jokes hey! I mean you can be silly if you want.
Yeah man, I can be silly only when you choose to.
Ah... I know where you going with this, and I am not going to entertain it.
Lol, ah, look at you, now you are the one who is reading my thoughts.
I am doing so because you started reading mine first.
Mmmmm... I do not read your thoughts, I know your thoughts and you know what? In fact I remember your thoughts. That's all you have to do, just remember my thoughts and you can make what you call quick rational decisive thoughts of imaginative memory. I am telling you all of this because I remember what you did as in like what I did. And just look at us, we are getting carried away again, and that's only because I enjoy your company, and you enjoy my company too, lol.... Man we enjoy our company, our company is the best ever. Man it takes two to tango. You see now you are making me think and wonder how life would be without me and you? How would life be without me as old Thato and without me as young Thato? Now that is very interesting, and funny enough I have the answer to it as always. And this answer I remember telling it to you a few pages back, and the answer is that it is and will be boring without either of us, it will be boring because there is Nothing to do when alone. You see I am also remembering stuff that I already know and have remembered, and it actually feels weird because as the older you, I am expecting myself to know better... but you know what? The good thing is that I remembered, and that is the important part.
Ahhrrg... lol, you are just defending yourself because you forgot hey.
Yes I did forget. I forgot it because you forgot it, but I remembered on your behalf, and I suggest you should also do the same. Come, let me and you remember what I did or what I am when I am forty. I know what I am when I am forty, but you have forgotten and I would like you to remember how your life is when you are at that age of forty.
Wow, now that seems a bit difficult, but then I guess I should not see or limit it to be difficult, because as you have always been saying throughout

these notes, that I am a living thought and what I actually think myself to be or see, I actually am that which I am and see. In other words I am my own thoughts, wow I actually am. So now as to answer your question, I believe and feel comfortable from all knowing that you have presented to me here now, that all I have to do is to go back or forward, whichever way it may be, and that is to say I have to imagine myself being forty, create and present myself with all the necessities that I wish and would like to have when I am forty. But this does not make sense considering that it will be more like I am prophesying about myself or my future, wow... wait, or even the past for that matter.

Yes indeed my son, you will be prophesying about your future or the past, and you know what? That is exactly what a prophet does, and that's what you are all doing now. A prophet can see the most truly held and beloved or treasured thoughts that you think yourself to be from your imaginative memory that you are. You see Thato my son, a prophet just like you as you are now, knows that everything is possible and even the impossible. Yes... yes... yes... again I know you have a question or thought to mind or a mind to thought, and I am explaining it now just for your pleasure my son. Now let me tell you this. That which you call a prophet even though you are one as well now, knows that the impossible is possible, you know this as well. You see, a prophet knows that you can change your mind just as he or she does and can change mind. He or she knows what you know, he or she knows that you can walk out of a house going to work, school, church, or just to your car, and just on your way you spot or see an ice cream stand, with a person that sells it. At that very instant or moment you then think of how it would actually be if you could taste, feel and indulge in a nice cold chocolate iced cream. You start to think and realize how hot or high the temperature of the day is. Which in turn gives you more reasons of your realized reasoned reality that you have thought from your imagination of memory to be true and vital to purchase the ice cream before your sight. And that is the moment when you will decide whether to buy one or not to buy one.

In deciding on buying or getting yourself an ice cream, you thus change and redirect from what you originally set out to do. As you are getting an ice cream you might also find interest in a young hot lady passing by, and even talk and ask for her number. While all of this is occurring, you have stored in your memory, what you set out to do at first. You see, it does not matter at what moment will it be that you decide to go back to your memory, and remember what you were doing before you saw the ice cream stand. The important part is that you will remember. The only delay in you remembering what you set out originally on is when you enjoy chatting or conversing with the lady and she also finds you interesting as well. Heck you even bought her an ice cream if that is the case. And she might even seduce you to come to her place with her and have a little bit of fun, which you are most likely to agree to. And by this time, Thato has forgotten that he was going to work, school, car, and church or meeting and so forth. Now also there is this part, you can and may decide consciously knowing that by agreeing to go with the lady will derail and delay you from what you were supposed to do originally, you can choose the newly created aspect of this new moment, and the other one you will knowingly resume to it later by choice.

This is what a prophet knows, and he or she can see it all, just as you have seen it all happen and decided for it all to happen in that manner you have chosen it to be through your thought. Now here is where it all gets a bit confusing, you Thato my son as a prophet that you are now, you know....

Wait... wait... just hold up here for a bit. I am not a prophet okay, yes I also know what you are going to say to me next. You see just like you, I also know you as well. I have been with you on these notes for a while now and I have observed, learned or as you would put it, remembered how you do, operate and go about things. You will tell me that I am a prophet just by simply imagining, thinking or creating myself to be where and what I chose to be, and the only way for it to be realized or manifested to be true, is to just fulfill or follow my first thoughts of imagination without thinking something else from what I have originally set or ventured on. Again in very simple words, you are telling me that I should just follow what I think, and it will be true, and so far it has been true, well I should say most of it, because I also think most of it not being true or real. This is what you would tell me.

Now in order to support your statement, I would have to think of something, or see myself doing something that I would like. I would have to think of something down or up forty years from now on. In doing so or saying so, I would then have to remember to keep to my words or vision all the time. I would have to make sure that whatever I do is in line with what I thought or saw myself in a self-vision and created prophecy. I would have to keep to this all the time, and every time as not to alter it. Now I am asking you older Thato, How is visioning myself being something that I am not now a prophecy? Actually you know what? You do not need to answer this one as well, because I can see your thoughts, just as you have with mine. Again I will answer it for you. You are about and you will tell me that, visions or a sight is a prophecy because once I vision myself being something that I am not now, I would first have to imagine it and think it through, as you have said that I am a living thought being, and that means that my visions are my thoughts. So whatever my visions are, they are my thoughts, since I imagine it first. And also what you are saying is that my imaginations that I strongly believe in will be true, this is what you have said and told to me, and this is what you would tell me now.

Mmmmhhhh..... Thato my son, I love you so much, and I love your confusions because they are mine. I was also once confused but now I am good and good I am. So far you have spoken for me, you have said what I would have told you, that is how much you are remembering. Now I can also sit, relax and just listen to you tell me what I think, and yet at the same time you refuse and deny that, by you reading or thinking with or for me is prophesying me or for me. But I know it is okay, and that it is never not okay. I just love myself the way you are. Now I would like it for you to please me by telling me what you think, see, vision, imagine, prophesy and finally remember yourself to be when you are forty. I would like to hear that which I already know from myself as yourself, I would like it for you to play around with me, change my ways by thinking and imagining me as already created.
Okay then, let me answer you by telling and sharing what you already know.
Yes please my son, tell me.

Now please do remember.
Okay, here I go. I have two children...ahm... nope man, I have eight children actually. You know what? This is not going to work man.
Oh... no please go on I am listening young Thato.

55

Hhhhmm... okay. I have a son, his name is also Thato, I have named him that, and his mother has agreed on this as well. Wow I can tell you this now, I love my son, and he has grown to be something so special. Lol, you know what, he actually reminds me when I was as young as he is now. He can be naughty at some times, but he is a very good child. Ahhhhh... man, as for my daughter.... Phheeww, now she is something else, she is so beautiful. Her beautiful brown eyes just remind me of her mother. I would have loved to call her Thatohatsi, but the mother was, "like no babe you cannot have a son and a daughter with almost similar names". But the truth is that they are not similar.

Would you please translate these names to English my son.

Okay cool, I will. First we will start with Thato. Thato means (will). It is the power and ability to will anything, just as it is with the will of God, it is will power or you can just simply say will creator. And Thatohatsi means Beloved, it is the precious and closely held love, it is being Loved. It is Beloved. And I love my children, and I think every parent does love their children.

And how is your wife?

Wow, my wife is just an awesome beauty man. I love the feel of her long hair, the smooth light skin and her smile when she stares right straight at me. I have made her quite upset at some times, but never the less she is very understanding of me. She has accepted me for whom and what I am. She would say to me at times,"Thato I love you", and wow how good it is to hear those words, "I Love you", from your partner in love crime.

Wow... Thato, that was and is beautiful my son. And it sounds like you have a happy family there going on for yourself. Wow, well done my son, I am so proud of you.

Lol. Thank you. So is it true that I have a wife and two children?

Yes it is true!

But what if it does not happen or turn out that way, then what?

Well it has happened considering that you have imagined it, but you can keep it on hold for a while until you remember it again that you actually have two children and a fabulous wife. You see, you can change it all now at once by thinking yourself as having eight children, heck you know what? You have had eight children. You enjoy having two children more than eight, and you rather have the experience of two children again than eight.

56

So tell me, are they going to have the same names that I mentioned above?

You tell me Thato, and I mean tell yourself Thato. You can change their names now if you choose to. You can even change your name now if you choose.

Yes I know that I can change my name now, but I now love the name Thato.

Do you even know what your name is?

What do you mean? You have been calling my name throughout these notes, and I just told you what it meant.

What I am saying is how sure are you that your name is Thato?

Well my mother gave me that name.

So you mean that anything your mother wished to have named you could have been your name?

Ahm... yes, she was the one who was highly authorized to do so at that moment of time.

So this means that your name might not have been Thato depending on what she would have named you right?

Yes it would or could not have been Thato if she had chosen otherwise.

So can I call you chicken head?

Chicken head! Why chicken head? My name is Thato man.

Lol, lol. Yes I know that, but who gave you that name?

I told you that my mother did.

What if she would have named you chicken head?

Then I would be chicken head. And if I really did not like it, I would change it.

So you would change your name as many times as you choose if you are not happy with it?

Lol, yes I would, I mean it only costs a few bugs to change my name on my ID.

Okay, let us now be more serious, and continue on our discussion. We will again revisit this name and naming of things. I will explain how things are named, and how they become about.

You have remembered.

I have remembered.

I tell you this, you are a prophet and I mean all of you are prophets of your own life, and your own life consists of many other. When I say other, I mean people and all other things that are sharing the now choice of thought with you, this is you and you are all of it. So yes, you are a prophet, and you may accept or reject what is, it still does not change what is, and what is, is everything. Now you know your family, you can spend time with them…. but before we explain this, I would like to get to your next question.

Okay, I am on it.

Do you think that I am an animal? I mean, what is the difference between an animal and a human? Am I more special than animals? Please, I would like to hear your take on this?

Oh wow… how I like the way you have phrased it. You have asked me of what I think. Think, think, and think once more is the important used word here. By you using the term think, shows that you are fully coming to remembrance, because there is Nothing we can do besides to think of how we would like to perceive that which is in our memory my son. Now I can tell you what I think, and what I think is what I know. I will tell you what I think, you are no different from an animal my son, in fact you are one. When I say one, I do not mean that you are it, I mean that you are all one thing perceiving yourself differently, and you have given yourself different names for each perception of thought being.

Okay, please tell me why you think so.

Oh yes I am. But first I would like to hear from your thoughts.

Okay, I personally do not think that I am an animal, I mean I can drive a car, operate a machine or computer, I stay in a good conditioned building that protects me from harmful animals and people. I can read, talk and I can cook proper food, and I have intelligence that an animal does not have.

Mmmmhhhhh….. That is very interesting, so you think all of that makes you anyhow better than that which you call an animal?

Yes, I do not see how it does not. I mean an animal cannot perform, be or do any of the above mentioned.

Okay good, you also know that there are some people who do not have a shelter to protect them, and also have nowhere to go but to sleep in on the streets right? Some people cannot read or speak as you do, but can be trained and taught to read or speak as you do just as with a monkey or a parrot has copied or learned. You do know that some people do not know how to operate machines, devices or gadgets of any sort and or even drive a car right?

Yes I do know that.

Okay, I tell you this, you are no different from animals, in fact you are just as much pretty petty the same, you are an animal. You see, that which you have called animals know themselves to be what they are, they can see and are aware at that moment of what they are, and thus they become what they have realized. Again do not worry or be troubled or confused, I will explain in details what I mean by this.

That which you call an animal appreciates and acknowledges their surroundings. It knows what a tree is, it knows what a flower is, it knows fresh water that flows from mountain streams back to the ocean, it knows that there is sun light, moon light, dark, bright, and it even knows that there are other species just as it is. That which you call an animal knows that it does not need a car, TV, fancy furniture, clothes or even a mobile phone. It does not need any of these things because everything that which makes an animal has already been provided for.

What do you mean that everything that makes it an animal has already been provided for?

Well if that which you call an animal is hungry, it goes to find its good prey, it grazes on good pastures, and it finds fresh water and drinks it. That which you call an animal produces and does give birth to infants, and some have or produce them as an egg which is just as the same as a human sac, but you have chosen to name it an amniotic sac. An amniotic sac is the same as an egg. The differences are the layers of both respected thought perceived beings, which is, the other one is soft and transparent, and that is of a human or mammal as you would refer to yourselves when you feel to identify yourselves as one with animals. And the other one is hard and non-transparent, which is of an animal, and in the end they are both eggs. If an animal needs to relief itself, it does exactly that without any shame or hesitance because it knows that all the others also do the same thing. That which you call an animal knows that it does not need covering because there is Nothing to hide, all that should be covered has already been covered by its skin and fur, may it be hard, feathery or soft, it matters not.

But animals are just out of control man, they do whatever they want to do, and one female or male can mate with any and as many other of its same type and there is no problem in or to this.

Well, that which you call human also does this. Humans whether it is a male or female can and does sleep around with many other of its same while still committed to the other, but wait… humans have also taken it to another level. Humans have slept with that which they call animals, humans have made animal porn with their involvement in it. That which you call a human has and still does sleep with its infants, children, wife and not just one wife, cousin, spouse, daughter, son, father and or mother, humans have had intercourse with one another very closely related. That which you call a human does the same things of that which you call an animal.

Mmmmm… That is very interesting, but I know all of this that you are telling and sharing with me now.

Yes I do know that you know, and I am bringing you to realization here slowly.

So would you say it is okay to sleep with my daughter?

Well I love your question again. And now I will ask you this, do you love your daughter?

Yes I do, I mean I do not have one now but I have one then.

Do not worry it does not matter, the fact is that you have a daughter.

Lol, okay.

You see love is very broad, and it is everything and all of it. Tell me, how do you love your daughter?

What do you mean? Is there a specific way of loving someone or something?

Oh yes indeed. When you say you hate someone or something it is because you love to hate them or it, you love that which you hate. Your love hate towards that thing is so strong that it upsets, destructs and boils you furiously intense from the love within.

Lol,lol. You know what you have just said does not make sense right?

Yes to you it does or may not, but I will explain it later to you. Right now we are still on the subject of whether you are an animal or not, and you still have not answered my question of how you love your daughter?

I just love her, I love her so much man.

Why do you not sexually sleep with her then if you love her so much?

No man, she is my daughter for God's sake! I cannot sleep with her, and it just does not feel right to me.

Okay fair enough. Do you think your daughter is beautiful? Do you think o have you noticed that she has nice firm fresh legs and thighs, and have you seen or noticed how nice and round her breasts and or ass is?

Yes I have noticed that, I mean she is my daughter, I raised her, I know her. But the way you are going on about it just seems and sounds sexual.

Well I tell you this, it only seems and sounds sexual because you have thought about it so, and you have thought it to be sexual... wow did you just think of your daughter in a sexual way Thato?

Lol, lol, well nope, but your words made me visualize it in that way.

Well I promise you that I did not mean it in a sexual way. I am just simply asking if you are aware, or if you have noticed your daughter?

Right now the way you look at sixteen and eighteen year olds... mmmhhhh.... That says a lot. You do not feel bad looking at a sixteen year old young girl in her mini skirt, in fact you love any woman from the age o sixteen to forty with a mini skirt on, that turns you on. Once you see a woman in hot pants and minis, you go crazy, you imagine all the things you could do to her, you have a blood rush flow to your penis.

Lol, man you do know me hey! That's just crazy man, you are creepy. Are you stalking me?

How can I stalk myself when I am with myself all the time?

So you mean that I am my own stalker?

Yes you are my man.

Okay, I see and yes I do agree that is how I feel when I spot a woman or a girl in hot pants or minis.... Oh and even nice cleavage as well, man that is just a turn on.

Yes I know it is for you. You have also seen and heard of a woman or a man getting married to their younger opposite sex with a huge age difference like twenty or thirty, and do you think all of this is wrong?

Well, I do not think so, I mean if they both consciously agree, I do not see why not.

Very good answer my son. So would you say if you and your daughter agree to marry each other it is okay then, since you love each other this or that much?

Well if you put it in that sense yes. But I do not want, choose, like, love, feel or fantasize of marrying my daughter, Thato!

Again, a very good answer of reply…. Then again, would you say that it is okay if a father and daughter or a mother and son have a thing for each other and decide to get married… you know what? Take the word marriage out of this, just tell me if it is okay for a parent and a child to have sex with each other if they both agree and they find each other attractive, and I mean sexually attractive, and also given the fact that they are both in love and aware of this?

Ahhhmmm…. Yes, I mean if they both feel comfortable with it, and they both have agreed on it, and this is what they both choose, I do not see why not. But this does not mean that a parent can have sex with their two months old babies, it does mean that they can have sex with their five, six, seven or ten year old children, because children do not know how to make beneficial decisions, they cannot decide on the good or bad.

Okay, first I will tell you this, thought is decisive, a thought is a decision, so whatever you think, you are. Do not forget that you are thoughts from imagination of your memory. Everything that you do, you first thought yourself doing it, you first imagined it, you then created it from your memory. Remember that I told you before you were born in this form you now know yourself, you were a thought?

Yes I do remember.

Sorry I just had to remind you here because you were forgetting. So a child, even a one minute year old baby makes decisions and choices. It decides when to sleep, it decides how and when to breathe, it decides to signal to its parent when it wants food, when it wants to pee, poop and play by crying. Again remember that there is a shared choice of thought. A shared thought you share it with people who you want and choose to share a thought with. So as you have thought yourself being a two year old child and have once imagined yourself having sex with your parent at that age, then so be it as it is with your thoughts, so be it as it is in your imagination of memory at this instant moment of time. I tell you this, be it that a child gets raped because it thought itself that way with the person it chose to experience with, and this could be the father, brother, mother or uncle, and it so because they love each other. Remember what a shared thought is my son, remember the story of a taxi driver and a worker or a student my son... please remember me and you. Remember!

Okay, I will remember.
Yes, please do! You see, because communicative relative love is a shared choice of thought, it is not fully understood, and hence I said before that a shared thought of choice is difficult to can see. Therefore it is difficult to accept what I will say next.
And what is that?
I tell you this, like I said before, animals know what they are, and they also know that there is Nothing to do but just to relate with each other. You see, because humans have set and rejected their feelings and emotions aside of how they feel about each other, and that is to say how they communicatively relatively love each or one another, they have caused themselves grief, jealousy and pain over one another.
I am not sure where you are going with this?
That is because you never let me finish what I am saying. You always interrupt me, just as you have interrupted your great thought about life by thinking it through many times as you have now chosen with your thoughts. You destruct your great thoughts by adding another different thought about that one thought you thought yourself to be... and please, I will again or make sense of what I am saying now later, okay.
Okay. So please then, continue.
Yes my son, because you so much see yourselves as not being animals, you then deprive the animal human you are from thought. I tell you this, there is no perfect relationship, all relationships are perfect. They are perfect because all and each single individual in a relationship has once or as many times created a thought about having sex with someone different other than their now current partner.

I tell you this, once you have remembered that you are all related, and that is to say that you are relatives the way you do not accept yourselves to be. If you were not related to anyone or even a stranger for that matter, you would not look at or like, talk to and or even have sex with

63

your husband, wife, girlfriend, boyfriend and or stranger. Your wife, husband, girlfriend, and or boyfriend was once a stranger to you. But now that you have come to relate with or to her or him, you have thus become relatives.

You see, I am explaining this communicative relative love to you now so that you may not judge a prostitute.

Wait, who said that I judge prostitutes?

Well no one, but you because you have just thought about it now and you are the one who is typing or reading this. You once thought and saw a prostitute as being filthy and immoral, and I do not blame you shame, because this is what was passed down to you as a thought. And now I am going to ask you this, have you ever slept with a prostitute?

Who me?!

Yes, you, who else would I be asking or talking to?

Okay I see, and I am also going to ask you this, what do you think?

I think and know that you have, remember that I am older than you and I know you better than you know me.

Well if you say, know and think so, then I suppose yes.

I am glad that you admitted it.

No seriously, tell me why you know and think that I have slept with a prostitute.

Well I tell you this, that girl that you met at church, bar, club and or on the street, is a prostitute just as you are as well.

And what if I or she is a virgin?

Well, you will then break it and pave the way for others to come.

And what if we both marry each other or maybe I would have married her and never have had sex outside our marriage, then what?

I tell you this, you do not know or remember that person's thought. Remember that what you think you create. A virgin can and may have thoughts of sleeping with someone, since the thought has been created, then the aspect has thus happened. That is why when the virgin finally decides and encounters the thought of sleeping with that one other that he or she so much desired for would say, wow, I have been waiting on this moment for a long time now, it is too good to be true and it feels so good. But he or she forgets that this has happened before by thought that was created by thy self. Even if you may suspect that he or she only by thought wants to get it down with other him or her, you still do not choose to see it that way as you think of it. And this is one of major reasons why people cheat. They cheat because they do not accept and understand themselves as attractively related to one another or each other. You as humans have refused to share love. You think that love is particular or peculiar to two persons or people only, and if it is more than just two it should not be the same as with the other.

I tell you this, husbands and or wives have left their houses during day or night time to see that one other special person. They have left the house or room because they would like to have a share of that good American pie or boerewors sausage that they so much desire to have. After having to indulge, they thus go back to their most favorite meal of all life time, and that meal is you back at home waiting and wondering about. You see, if both parties would understand that we are all relatives, and we share our choices of thought by being with each other, they would understand that they love and have the same feelings to the next person they choose to have with. For a person to try out a new different or same meal, it is because they have not had it for a long while or have not ever had it before, and there is really Nothing wrong with trying out that which you desire for this or that moment. Come on now Thato, do you wish and want to eat pap and moroho or burgers, or salads and greens for the rest of your life?

Lol, heck no!

And the truth is that you do get sick from one meal all the time.

So now I tell you this, do not as you can and will judge a prostitute because they have made a shared choice of thought to fulfill your choice of you cheating on your wife and or husband or friend to have your sexual pleasures and desires met. And I promise you that the girls you have met at church, bars, restaurants, clubs and or hotels are and were prostitutes. You say and think that it is better for you to not know that a girl or a woman sell themselves. So for you it is okay even if it is or was a prostitute that you had sex with, as long as you did not know and did not pay for that one night, then it is okay! I tell you this, it does not change the fact that she is and was a prostitute and that you bought her drinks and even took her out for dinner one time to make a payment to her in one different form from the traditional payment of paying for prostitutes…. And you are a prostitute as well as much as she is because you have left your kids and wife or girlfriend with no kids to have sex with a woman that has a husband and kids or a girl with no kids. You see, someone or the next person can do or think the things that you always think of through your thought of imaginative memory as well. You should understand that imagination is for everybody and not only for you, because if you imagine that you are the one who is imagining things the way you imagine them, therefore this means that you think you are the only one capable of doing that. And this is not true because we share our choices of thoughts, and our thoughts are in our imaginative memory that we all are. So you are a prostitute because she once caught you on bed doing your sexual thing with that other one her. You are a prostitute because he once caught you on bed doing your sexual thing with that other one he. I remind you again, do not think that you are the only one that can imagine doing this or that, because imagination is for everybody, then the next person can imagine doing this or that. I tell you this, if you really love, like and enjoy, and that is to say that if your favorite dish or food is prawn curry, there is Nothing wrong with eating fish today and tomorrow crave for meat, and the next day eat vegetables. I mean if the food is good, then it is good hey? Why stop what is good? But this does not mean that you are cheating on prawn curry, you still do love prawn curry with all your heart, but your taste is not only prawn curry, you also like to try out good new food or craving, and also know that there are some other people who love prawn curry just as you do or even more. I tell you this, prawn curry is for everyone and anybody who loves it. But do beware and make sure that the food you eat is not poisonous or harmful to your health. So yes, accept now that, that one person you so much love is not for you only. There are many other people who love that person as much as you do or even more. That person is for everyone and anybody who loves him or her. Share your love in plain sight. Share your love with your brother, mother, father and sister, because you are all related.

So are you saying that all the girls that I have slept with are prostitutes? Well I tell you this, you are crazy to think that you are the first and or the last. I mean they were with or were sleeping and having sex with someone for a very long now before they met you in their imaginative memory. You see, just as with the girls you have met, prostitutes also sleep and have sex with you now, and I mean for a very short brief now. So in a sense a

66

prostitute is your girlfriend at that or this moment of time now because you are relating and loving each other sexually now or then. After you are done with loving each other sexually with that prostitute, you then break up instantly and move on to the next prostitute or wife and or girlfriend. So now I tell you this, as long as you stop your friendship or relationship with someone, you thus break up the friendship or relationship. It is a relation because you relate with that someone or person or thing at that or this moment, and it will be a break up until you decide to get back together again and thus relate once more the way you choose to. And also I tell you this, that prostitute that you see and observe on the street is someone's mother, father, brother or sister and or daughter or son. They have chosen to give you sexual pleasure in order for them to lay and set food on the table. So how dare you judge the profession and skill that you privately do in your rooms and houses. How dare do you Thato my son! You have given names to prostitutes. You call them bitches, whores, sluts and or dogs. Well I tell you this, you are also that. You are a bitch, whore, slut and or a dog because you have changed so many woman and girls in your life and or including prostitutes because you have serviced all of them the same, and they all to you the same as well as they have thought themselves to be just as you have.

So now how should I look at my friends?

The way you want and always have looked at them.

Okay I see.

And now I tell you this!

You are addicted to a drug.

You are an addict. You are a substance abuser. You cannot go without a moment without having to crave for what you are addicted to.

Me?! An addict? I am not an addict. I do not use drugs, heck nor have I ever touched any.

I tell you this, you are an addict to life.

Aaaahhhhhhhh... man, come on. That is just not fair, and it does not make sense.

I promise you it does! I tell you this. You are addicted to life so bad and so much, that you do not will, wish, want and choose to stop using it. You love this drug called life so much and dearly, that you are even scared of losing it. Remember that an addiction is something that you are used to, and cannot live without. You are so much addicted to life that you cannot live without it. You have abused this substance called life in so many ways that you cannot comprehend it. You have sexed your lives away and thus have you been diagnosed with diseases and illnesses. You have eaten life away, and thus you are fat and obese or have gout. And you have drank your life and smoked it, thus you have cancer. And also you have abstained life away, and thus have you died anyway from old age and killed life away! This is how much you love to abuse life, you abuse it because you enjoy using it as a substance, you cannot abstain from life, that is how much you love it. You even go for counseling in order to get help and an understanding on how to use this substance called life. Now in your time you have psychologists, people who specialize in helping those who do not know how to use this substance called life properly. You are not aware that even a counselor or psychologist is addicted to life as well. He or she is also trying to light up this thing called life so that he or she can smoke it, and once it is done, they buy another pack, in doing so, you are reaped off because you pay for what they have to tell and say to you.

Okay, so what should I do as not to abuse life or use life?

Nothing!

I have remembered.

You have remembered.

Wow, that was just a bit deep and tense, I should mind what I think hey! Otherwise I could lead myself to self-destruction.

Yah, tell me about it, it was too deep hey. Oh yes indeed you should mind my son. I liked it when you used the word beneficial. You said that a child cannot make beneficial decisions. And you know what? All of you are beneficial to each other, and that is why you always share a thought together. You are a shared thought, all your relationships are beneficial to all of you. Your relation with your mother is also beneficial, even if you are adopted, you are also benefiting from adopted parents. A parent, whether he or she adopted a child or not, is willing to give and do sacrifices for his or her child. You as a child your benefits are free food, clothes, toys, money and so forth. All that your parent has worked for is beneficial to you, and that is why you will be left a will, and a parent does this out of love. A parent benefits from a child things such as getting chores done, getting good grades from school and then finally get work just as the parent did. These are just simple benefits, the most important benefit of all that I have to mention is love. Yes indeed it is love, because a parent may not work, and a child may not do chores or get good grades and work just as the parent did, and when this happens, it is when communicative relative love occurs. You see when you have no work, chores, school or duties there is Nothing to do but to bond with each other, and decide what should be done together, and you can bond with each other by talking, touching, feeling, intercourse and knowing each other, and this we call communicative relative love. The way you communicate and relate creates love. That is why you would find that which you call animals sitting and relaxing under the sun or shade of tree licking, touching, playing and feeling each other or mating. You see, animals know that there is Nothing to do but relate with themselves and or to each other. Animals know that they do not need material stuff to live, and they do not need anything to make their lives easier as their lives are already easy. Land animals are not concerned of traveling overseas because they understand that they are already over the sea, it does not matter which side they are on because the land on that side, is over the sea, and the land this side, is over the very same sea. This communicative relative love is exactly what we have been talking about here, you use it in the tool of recorded music or writing as we have mentioned. Animals do not have a problem with having to mate in close family line, like a parent and its child. They understand communicative relative love better. They do not deny, judge or dislike who or what they are. That which you call animals know there is Nothing to do but to love one another, animals know that they benefit from each other. A lion knows that it will benefit a good meal from a springbok, a springbok knows it will benefit a good grassy meal from the bush, the grass knows that it will benefit good nutritional mineral meal from the soil, water and sun. And soil knows that it will benefit good water inevitably because land is connected to water, water knows that it is formed from hydrogen and oxygen, and it also knows that it does not need hydrogen or oxygen to be water because it was never water before. It knows it was never anything, and therefor does not need anything but just to be water. That which you call animals know that they do not need anything but just to be animals, they know they need to be an animal in order to become an animal. That which you call humans think that they

69

need a car, home, bed, and or money to become a human. It thinks that it needs clothes, and fancy things that are material to become humans, and the irony is that humans never had these things before, but they thought themselves intelligent and thus have created their intelligence. All that they have now is all made up from desired thought of intelligence as they have thought. Oh wow but they never think that you need a human to be human. And what makes you that which you call human? What makes you human is that you eat, drink, sleep, fart, poo, urinate, cry, think, talk or make sounds and reproduce. That is what makes you human as you now are. This is what you call a human. But wait, wait, wait, how is all of that or this different from animals? Animals also experience things that humans do and feel.

I tell you this, you and animals are the same.
Animals kill, and humans kill!
Animals eat other animals including that which you call human and vegetation. Humans eat animals and vegetation, and some humans eat other humans. I tell you this, this is not different from that which you call an animal.
You think that being a vegetarian is good and healthy. You justify yourself by saying that you do not want to eat that which has been brutally killed and slaughtered against its will. You say you feel sorry for that poor animal, oh that poor chicken or cow. I tell you this. You should be feeling sorry for that carrot you are eating, you should feel sad on how you chop and cut that poor spinach. You do not realize that whatever you eat, you eat it against its will on your will.
So are you saying that eating vegetables is a bad thing as well?
Nope, I am not saying that! I am just making you realize the other thing here. You have forgotten that, trees, plants and all vegetation is alive. It does not mean that if something does not talk, and it's just standing still like a tree of fruits, it should be eaten. But still you choose to eat it against its will, you do this because it does not say anything, it does not say, "hey please do not eat me sir or Mr.!" In this you assume that it is okay to eat vegetables and all that is green. You think that eating meat is bad, my man you do not even know how bad it is to eat vegies.
Is it bad?

Nope! You can only eat that which you like, and remember that what you like, you are. And remember that you are that which you eat. You eat what you can. What you eat will kill you. And also Nothing will kill you. And I mean it, Nothing will kill you, oh it will kill you. So if you feel sorry for that chicken then you should have the same feelings to that carrot, potato, tomato, spinach and so forth. If you cannot raise a knife to a chicken, then do not lower a hand to uproot that carrot or spinach. Do not cut down that poor old long standing tree just to make your homes and have nice warm fires during winter. Do not walk on that grass, do not cut flowers and roses just for a special few hours of Valentine's Day.
But that spinach or carrot will waste away if I do not eat it mos!
Yes indeed, and that animal will waste away if you do not eat it mos!
Okay, understand, so it does not matter what I eat?
Yep!
So then what should I choose to eat then?
I tell you this, eat breath.
Now that does not make sense.
Well sure it does, you are doing it right now by breathing, if you eat breath you will know how to live. Do not worry, all of this will make sense once I explain everything that you wish to ask me, and think to ask. Do not worry my good friend, be patient you will know, you will remember all that which you are.
Okay, Mr. Smart guy continue then.
Hey, hey, hey, take it easy there, I am not trying to be smart here now, I am answering your thoughts about your thoughts.

Now I would like to remind you of a shared thought again. This time you will remember both memories that I have used to remind you of how you relate with thoughts being, how you relate with others, and I mean others like that which you call animals.
I will share with you now of how a poodle met with its human friend.
Lol, okay this should be very interesting Thato.
Wait for it Thato, listen first and then you may decide if it is of your interest or not.

There is and was once up on a moment of imaginative memory of poodle dog and its human friend. The poodle was very young and homeless, its poodle dog mother and poodle dog father had moved somewhere to the country because they were spotted while scratching through bins for food, and taken to animal care and were later adopted by humans. So this left little young poodle as an orphan on the big streets of the city wondering about. But young little poodle dog was very wild with imagination, it wanted to live in a nice big fancy house, with a huge yard, swimming pool, sleep on a nice bedding and wake up to good food, travel the world in private jets and meet other famous dogs, it wanted that which you call the good life. It had a strong believe on its imagination, it saw it true and possible. And indeed it was and is possible.

And so as it was and as it is with young poodle dogs' thoughts.

Not so far now or then was a young human girl. Now she had that which you call wealth and riches, she had it easy and she knew it, anything that you desire, she would buy or own it. At one moment of time she and her parents went to the city to do some shopping. While walking to different stores she noticed a young poodle dog, right then here and now, she saw the dirty young poodle wondering about, and sniffing about.

You see, the had been many passing by and noticing the poodle, all loved it, all adored it, but each of all wanted to give to the poodle that which the poodle wanted and desired, and they did not have it as they have thought themselves to being. They felt and imagined the things they would give to the young poodle if it was theirs, but in their knowing thoughts of imaginative memory, they knew that they did not have the things they would like to give to the poodle, and that which the poodle desires. That is why it was left alone so that it can fulfill its dreams.

And so as it is as it should be.

The young girl called out to the parents, "mommy, daddy look! It's a nice little poodle, oh how cute it is" she said. She loved it and was willing to buy no for the young poodle.

She rushed after it, and caught up with it.

When she saw how cute it is, she smiled, and so did the young poodle. They both smiled because in their deepest knowledge of heart they knew that they were fulfilling what they imagined. It was not so long after that, that the poodle was spotted on TV with the girl, it was on magazine covers, it travelled around in private jets and was treated like a queen or king just as it thought itself it would be one day. It had some of that which you call the best luxury. It had all the things that which most humans love and desire.

I am sharing with you this just to remind you that whatever you think at this instant of now, someone is also willing to fulfill your thoughts just as the same as with the story of a taxi driver and a student or worker.

I tell you this, if a poodle can own so much without doing anything, how is that all different from humans? I tell you this, that poodle is a Queen and or a King, and the little girl is a slave and or servant to the young poodle, because she is doing all the work while the poodle does Nothing!

So are you saying that if I own a pet, I am actually a slave to it?

Well I tell you this. You have to make sure that, that pet is clean, fed, clothed and well taken care of, and even protect it from harm as you have dedicated and obliged yourself so, just as you would to a King and or Queen. If that which you call an animal can have it easy!

Now imagine what you can do!

Iyoh, iyoh, wow… wow… pphheewww.

Yah, believe it!

Now that you are wide clear on how you connect and communicate with each other by means of recording and leaving pieces of you everywhere as a shared memory, you go for or to someone to notice or acknowledge your existence. We can now move on back to what you were saying about you loving people equally the same.

Okay, lol, I see you have not forgotten. Yes we can my dad.

Earlier you said that you love people all the same just as you love your mother, and you also said that however you do not like or you hate their behavior and attitudes, this is what you said. But I know how you feel and what you meant to say, that is why me and you are going to look, listen and read this out clearly so that you may and can understand. I know your feelings, I know your feelings very well because they are mine, I am feeling you Thato my son, I know you very well, I can see you very well, I can touch and hear you super clear. Since I know you, I will tell you who you are and what makes you. Yes indeed it is true that you do not judge, but we should say that you at maximum level try not to judge people or someone, but if you look at this carefully one can say that it is impossible not to judge. Yes, yes, yes I do know that impossible is the limit that you have set yourself considering that you can do things to a certain extend and from there forth the rest is just impossible for you, and this does not make sense when knowing that impossible is Nothing and everything is possible including the impossible. Now then, when you make an observation or when you become aware of something, that means you are judging what you are observing, you are judging what you are aware of.

This confusion can be better explained by giving one known simple typical practical example. When you cross the road, you always make sure that the road is clear or it is safe to cross. But how do you make sure of it, how do you know when and when not to cross? Well for sure you have to observe what is going on around your surrounding and on the road, you observe if it is clear of traffic or not, this is what you do. In doing so, that is to say after observing, you make a judgment of when to cross, how to cross and at what pace to can cross with or at. Another argument can be brought forward, another person may say but what if I choose not to cross, what if I choose to go back to the direction I came from or what if I just stand there forever and not cross the road but simply observe the traffic, and see the traffic by me? How is that a judgment? And one will be right in raising such an arguable question. And I will tell you this, any decision is a judgment by thought. See if you wait there forever, you will be aware of other things than just traffic. You will be aware of people, trees, birds and the small environment around you. So this means there will be destructions because you may see a girl or a lady in a mini skirt and you may feel that wow she is hot, hot will be your judgment of that young or old woman in a mini skirt passing by. You may even notice that which you call a homeless person, and think to yourself that, that is not how you would like to end up because you will have made a judgment that it is not good for you to be like that. So then do realize if you avoid any single judgment, you open yourself to wide more ranged judgments around you.

Okay, that is well explained. So would you say I should not judge a book by its cover metaphorically speaking?
Mmmmhhhhh…. Now that is one of your famous interesting questions, and guess what? Lol, I love it.

Yes I know you love my questions, and it seems that you always get excited because you know you have the answer to them or it.

Yes my man it is that easy. Come on I am sure you can hit me harder than that. Throw me with some stones, or you know what? How about you hit me with a comet, actually hit me with a planet man. Lol. And if that is not enough, try me with the universe Thato my man.

Woah…. Woah… whoah, you are getting way too full of yourself Mr.!

Oh yes I am full of myself, in fact if that is the case, I am full of you Thato. You have filled me with yourself completely, I have joy, love, understanding and everything because of you Thato my son, I am high on your life. You are the most beautiful thing that has ever happened to me as Thato from you Thato my son.

Okay cool, I understand. Would you please answer my question.

Sure I will and I am. You see, what you have asked is very broad, but I will explain it to you in the simplest form that you have so far understood from our entire notes here. I tell you this, like I have said earlier that it is impossible not to judge, and also it is possible not to judge….." Impossible is possible, if impossible is possible then possible is equal to impossible, possible is impossible." And this confusion of words I will better explain it as we come closer to the end of these notes, for this moment of this imaginative memory that you are here now on, it is okay.

Okay proceed, I am listening.

I tell you this, yes do judge a person and do judge not a person.

So what are you really saying, you merely not saying anything here man.

Wait for me Thato. I tell you this, you can judge a book by its cover because that is exactly what you see, you are not at fault in observing and judging what is on the cover, and also you are not at fault in opening the book and finding out what is inside the book and making a judgment of what is inside the cover of the book itself. I tell you this Thato, remember that you are a thought being from imaginative memory, everything that you are you have thus thought yourself to be. Some thoughts you produce instantly while some others you produce them in a distance of space, space can be close, short, long, far or far faraway, it all depends on that. So if you happen to spend a moment sharing a smoke or a beer with someone… are you wrong to assume or judge that that person smokes or drinks beer on the regular? Well for sure not. And I tell you this, because that person has imagined and thought him or herself trying out drinking and or smoking at that moment, it makes him or her a smoker. He or she is not a smoker only if she or he is not drinking or smoking at that moment. You see Thato my son, you choose to be this and that every moment of time, and you are this and that every time you do this and that. If someone finds you not with a glass of beer now, that simply means you are not drinking now, and you can choose not to drink beer forever now, and you can change forever now to drink beer now.

Yes, yes I understand…. You see, if or when someone is like this or that, and you observe and see this or that, how can you be wrong or at fault to judge or assume that, that particular person is like that or this at that or this moment? I tell you this, you are who you are at this or that moment which you feel now, and do trust me that you my good friend can feel anything you create from you thought being of imaginative memory now. So I tell you again, do judge and do judge not a book. Lol, here is the funny part, do judge only that which you see now!! And what can or would you see now? I tell you this, you would see this or that now.
Look around you my son and tell me what you see. I tell you this, you see what you are seeing now and what is now can change now to anything that now is. Yes my good loving friend, son, daughter, brother, father, mother, uncle and all that you can call yourself, you are who you are now. To can know who you are now, do take a moment and observe yourself, see yourself now, and tell yourself who you are now and you will see who you are! I know that you are imagining it now. And I know how it feels… and this is how it feels.
Wow..wow…woahh… woah… hoah…. Is this really me, what am I now? Oh my good lord I am that which I am right now! Now I am sober, now I am tipsy, now I am drunk, now I am a killer, now I am angry, now I am stupid, now I am happy, now I am sad and now I hate you and myself for hating you! How am I now? I really feel good of who I am right now because now is here, I am with now and now is with me. And all of this feels so, so, so good.
This is exactly of how you feel about now, and now is legendary, legends are made now, now is your biggest memory of all now time!
Wow, okay old Thato, I hear you. Wow now that was really good. I do not know where it came from, but it felt good to let all now out… damn I got to give it to you older Thato, you are good with words, you know how to

turn me on, you fill me up like Nothing in the universe, I really just had a taste of food for soul. I am cheered up my man, and therefore I thank you for it. I thank you for being this awesome Thato.

You have remembered Thato my son.
Thank you for appreciating me as who you really are Thato. Therefore I really thank you for yourself, I love you again and again my son. Words my not truly express how I feel about you, therefore I will say that I really love feel you man.
Mmmmm…. Yes I have remembered.
Okay let's calm it a bit down here, otherwise we sound super gay right now.
Hah… gay? Really, are we going to talk about that as well?
Lol, I meant gay as in happy… oops, your mind is lurking with thoughts hey?
I have a question for you older Thato, are you gay?
I am always gay!
Lol, come on man, answer the question.
Lol, the fact that you are thinking about it now, you might just turn me into one now.
Lol, I see. So it is all first by thought and the rest is history, and now is just what is now. And now I am not gay and I can forever be now and or I can change now at any moment of now, right?
My man you have got it, spot on boss!
This is what I get from most people. People do judge, assume that I am gay and no matter how I explain that I am not, it is still not enough. I mean I really do think that I know myself. I mean if someone sees and feels themselves as being that which is called gay, I really do not have a problem with that. Sorry older Thato, I am going to do a little bit of talking here, so please give me a chance.
It is all good, go ahead my son.
You see we live in a stuck up world that denies itself to be what it is. I mean I do not have a problem with anyone who is gay, it actually does not hurt me a bit, it does not matter, and I really do not care man. I do not have a problem or see anything wrong with holding a guy's hand or holding him around the hips, yes it sometimes feels funny because I was brought up that men should not touch men in that way or manner. And I

am sure that my very good friend Andrei Damane knows this as well. Well I feel and think that if you do not believe me, then you should ask Andrei Damane. And you know what? I hate rules so much because they restrict who I am as Thato. Actually come to think of it, why is it not wrong or seen as bad for a grown son to slouch on his fathers' shoulder when he needs a shoulder to cry on? A father parent may kiss his grown son or nephew on the lips and still it is not seen as gay just because they are closely related. So rules can be bent when felt like it, especially if it is in the family. You know what also? I at sometimes feel like going to the beach with any one guy friend of mine and just chill and enjoy the sunset or rise if that is the case. But I always create these thoughts of that awkward moment when we are close to each other and he starts to think that all of this seems a bit gay for him, I know this because this is how I also feel at sometimes. I have a good friend of mine called J.C, he always says to me, "Thato bra, I miss you man, or Thato bra I love you dog but do not think I am gay." Even Thabiso Mokoena and Rudi also says this to me at times, but they feel so bad and ashamed of saying it, and they try to explain in what way they actually meant it. I really do not see or think of them being gay. I know them as my friends, I know my preference and theirs, and our preference is woman at this moment. Listen, I get some men who would like to have sexual intercourse relation with me, but that is not my preference. They all try, and most assume my being as being who I am now is gay. But damn I love my woman. A woman interests me a lot. If I would love the experience of a penis, I will feel mine, I have my own and I know how it is like to have a penis on me. Iyoh, have you seen a woman's figure in hot pants or miniskirts? Have you felt and heard how a woman moans during sex? Man that just turns me on. I love black dark complexioned woman... but I have really never been with one. I struggle so hard to have sexual intercourse relation with a super dark woman.

I love firm breasts, firm thighs and a little bit of an opening between the thighs and the vagina with a little bit of extra firm tight buttocks. If I could wake up every morning and venture on different sexy woman according to me just to explore what pleasures and stimulates them differently, that will give me real great pleasure. I do not mean to boast here or anything, but man I do not mind going for two days all the way with a woman. Well for sure there will be breaks, but as long as my little man still feels to go strong why not man? And to be honest with you Thato, I fully express myself to someone after having sex with them, I mean immediately just after sex, I am free to say this or that because I am not as shy as I was before we had sex. A lot of woman find me really fun after encountering sexual relation with me because the barrier of getting lucky or not getting lucky has been broken and no one between the two of us has to be conservative or self-withdrawn to be as they are before the barrier was imagined. People must just get along with each other as they are man, and they should just be who they are. Take a look at this older Thato. You know, sometimes when I am in a taxi or any place, and I am next or opposite to a woman that I find hot and sexy, I sometimes feel like saying," look lady, you are really beautiful and attractive to me now at this moment and I would really like and love to have sex with you. Would you mind to?" But I do not do this because of the society and environment I am in. I mean if you feel to have it with me now and I also feel the same, why not just do it and get rid of the feeling? What if I could be your next or previous lifelong partner? Why not just have fun with what you are feeling now as you. I mean sex is also an experience right? Nah man… people are not honest with their feelings about sex. Why take four or five days, two or six months, and or one or two years before you give it in and all up? And only in the reason of wanting to be sure of the person first, and afterwards to your disappointment of long wait to find out that he or she was just craving and wanting that only and even cheated on you, and only just as you have wanted it but procrastinated on it, only to find he or she just wanted that and Nothing else but that. I mean you could have had sex sooner and saved yourself time of guilt, pain and emotional self and counter betrayal. I think twice every time, actually I think five times or even more before I approach a woman because I have to create her reactions of anything that I would say to her and try to work on around what I am saying, and to be honest with you I am really not good with lines. People want to be picked up with a hot line and stuff, they do not go with what they most of the time feel. They want, hey baby, how is this? How is that? And this is this and that is that, just like that hey baby! And from that you will be judged if you are a winner or a loser.

You know what? I think we need more gay straight people. Once a gay person has fully accepted who he or she is, they embrace who and what they are, they get to be comfortable with whom they are and that is because they have chosen and they know who they are. So if you would get a straight woman who just freely makes moves, tells and hits on guys about how she feels without thinking first that she is a woman, and that is to say that as a woman you do not hit on guys or behave a certain way. I know you do get woman like that, but woman who approach men and in most cases they are judged as bad or wrong, and a person is really wrong for how he or she feels? Damn my creation man, it is not cool at all. Iyoh my man you should see how conservative African woman are, they will tell you my culture this and my culture that, and or how much they are worth because they are educated as if it is a new thing. They think that education is their value. But when you ask her or the person of how she feels about the whole thing, it is very contrary to her culture and or education. So in a way feelings are suppressed and ignored. Hell I would like to have sex with people who feel to have sex with me now. I get woman who would love to have sex with me now, but some and not all, do judge my height and status, and because of just these few simple things, it isn't happening tonight. Here in South Africa, women are just all about money and their security. If you got money, my man you have just said everything, you do not need to say a word, things will just happen for you. And I am sure they are like that in the States of America and some parts of the world as well. I mean that is what their music videos details, and you said that our grandest communicator of feeling is the music that is now. So yah, we need gay straight woman and gay straight man. I find men here as well just as much as the same as women. I mean a man finds it okay and cool to can cheat on a woman, but becomes furious when the woman does exactly the same. Men here where I am now also feel that as a guy you are the one who needs and has to approach a woman or a girl even if you both have a thing for each other, and women also expect that from men, and if you do not, then I am sorry my friend you are pretty much seen as a coward, or as a chicken standing on one leg.

You see older Thato, nowadays I do not even bother myself in chasing after girls. Oh no do not get me wrong here, I do look, I do desire... but I just let the moment happen man. When I am in a church, pub, club or bar, I am not going to chase after women, in fact I do not. Yes I do go for women and beer with music entertainment… but I just let the conversation carry or lead itself to us ending up being on a bed together and having fun sex in that heat of the moment, and afterwards go our respective chosen ways on the next moment if we do choose so.

Mmmmhh… I know and understand Thato my son, and that is why I stated very clearly that you should not judge a prostitute.

Lol, ah now I see… you are clever Thato, not bad at all for an old guy like you hey.

Well, and not bad at all for a young guy like you Thato my son.

Okay, check you later.

Sure.

Hello older Thato or young Thato, how are you doing today?

I am good my son, and I know that you are troubled.

Yes I am indeed. Today is this day, and oh boy am I not feeling done! I am tired my good friend, my body is done. I am really exhausted and extremely tired, I am worn out man. Mmmmmhhhh…. I am just down man, I do not know whom to talk to but you, well I guess I should say I do not know whom to talk to but me. I can try to explain or tell someone of how I am feeling right now, and even though they may understand because they have experienced such a feeling at one moment, but they would not truly understand because they would not be feeling it now. And so it seems that the only person who can truly understand what I am feeling right now is me. I am the one who is feeling and experiencing all of this right now, and the only best better person who can understand these feelings or this feeling of emotions is me, or you Thato. I rather come to you now here, and talk to you because you understand, you are me, and you are sharing with me that which I am now, you have been here once and you are here again Thato my good friend. I know that I have had this feeling many times before, even when I was way younger than I am now, and every time when I have it, it tells me to stop what I am doing and just be myself. And what do I really mean by this? I mean that, it tells me to make my own choices…. Yes I know I have been making my own choices all along and all the time, but it tells me to make my own loving choices, my own desired loving choices at this moment of now.

Right now I do not feel like going to work, I feel like quitting my job and just stop working. I really would love to put my body to rest from work... but wait, this thing pays my rent man, and it supports me with food, clothes me, and even pays my transport. If I quit now, how will I make it through? How will I keep myself entertained at my own desired will without having to ask anyone for a cent? I am used to supporting myself; I am used to being my own rigid structure since the age of eighteen. And also during the time of my mother being my supportive guardian and structure, I never really troubled her that much for money. I never wanted fancy things in general. I mean, I have never owned a bicycle Thato, a TV game or what you would now call play station, Xbox or a Nintendo. I can tell you this my good man, I never complained not even a bit about my life... I mean if I did complain, please do remind me because there might be some moments when I complained and I have now forgotten, but so far my memory serves me that I was happy all the time regarding my home situation and condition. Look, right now it does not mean that I am complaining, I am just simply reminiscing on the things that occurred in my child hood and teens. I also remember that on my birthdays, I was never thrown a party. I always knew what to expect, and guess what? It was always a cake, me and my mother and just three or a few more relatives. To be honest with you Thato Motchello, I do not mind having nice fancy things, and beautiful luxurious materialistic stuff, but I really do not care, I do not put them to heart, I do not walk around stressing for this or that. All I would love to have is a house that I fully own, a house that is not owed to the bank, a house that I choose, that I like, or I can even build it. I do not mind having a car, but I really do not care man. All I would like to have right now is just a simple house here right now or an apartment here in Cape Town and one in Bloemfontein. But then again who does not wish for these things? I really do not care about someone's riches. Why should I care of that which I do not now possess or own, why be envious of that which I do not have, why hate my brother or be jealous of that which my sister has? If there is any reason I should be feeling this way, please tell me now Thato. Please! You see all of this does not mean I do not have desires, I mean if I were to own or buy a car, oh trust me it would be a jeep. And not just any jeep, it has to be the classic wrangler of late 90s and early 2000... that is my favorite car, but I do not feel sad or bad in not owning or having one now. Lol, and every time when I spot a classic jeep wrangler, I go like, "yeah baby you are coming with me to or with me home."

Oh… my mother.

Oh my mother, do not think for a moment that I have forsaken you. Do not even for a moment think that I do not love you, do not in memory imaginatively think that I do not care of or about you. I love you dearly, I worship you, I am proud like a father to you. Your strengths have felt and lifted me up. You are the one who raised me, you are my teacher, and you have been and always are my way of path. I know that we do not communicate as you would have loved to, we do not communicate as expected, but oh my sweet mother, you are my mother, you are my all. I spent nine months connected to you by a cord, me and you have shared a breath and thoughts, me and you have shared pains, laughter and good moments like a chemical bond, or maybe an ionic bond. That is my connection to you. I may call every day, and ask how things are but that does not change how things are, I can tell you what to do and you can tell me what to do, but that does not change how things are. I can give you direction and advice, and you can give me direction and advice, but that does not change how things are. I can give you direction and advice and you can give me direction and advice and our moments and situation may be transformed from it, but it does not change how things are. I will always love you in this condition, in this situation. I love you in this moment of now of thought being imaginative memory mother. You have inspired me by giving birth to my life through your thoughts. I really do not know what more to say, if sex was and is the only way I would offer my love to you sexually, then that will show and is how I love you, but we, me and you know that sex is not the only way to express love. Love is and can be fully expressed by being, and now we are together oh sweet mother, let us be who we are. I love you so much that I would even make love to you. Because words are hard to believe, action is also hard and difficult to believe as I have remembered. So I tell you this mother, believe my feelings, believe my feelings oh sweet mother. For me to say more than that which I have now said, will be faulty and all made up. I have told you how I feel, and all you have to do is to feel and believe what you choose. And I have chosen you for a parent.

Thank you for being there, thank you for being here man. Thank you, thank you and thank you. You deserve all that I have given to you. Use it.

You have remembered.

I have remembered.

Mmmmmmmhhhhhh.... Wow Thato, you were really feeling something there hey!

Yah I was Thato my good friend.

I have been listening to your expressive feelings and how you see yourself Thato my son. I have thus strongly observed and became that which I was once through you. I tell you this, you have done well Thato, you have felt that which is a feeling. And this is what you used to struggle with, this is what many of you struggle with. I am going to share with you now something that you have experienced, I am going to tell you about feeling. Come closer my son, come closer my daughter, let us talk about feeling, yes, yes, and yes feelings. You see you do not have to be confused anymore, and you do not have to be in emotional despair my son, all of many of you can relax wherever you are now Thato my son.

Listen, I tell you this, every time when you feel sad, every time when you feel angry, all you have to do is to feel sad, all you have to is to feel angry.

Aahhhmmm.... I am not sure if I understand. What or how do you mean? Today you said that you are or were feeling sad and down about, you felt like quitting on what you now have right?

Yes that is exactly how I felt and feel.

Now then, when I say feel bad, I mean exactly that. I am telling you to feel bad, I am telling you to feel angry.

What are you talking about? I am telling and explaining to you that I am feeling sad and down, and you are telling me to feel exactly that which I am feeling, and I am telling you this that which I feel.

Yes! That is exactly what I said. If you feel bad, just feel bad. I mean have you ever tried feeling bad or down or angry?

Well I have not tried, but I have felt bad and down and angry, I have felt a lot of feelings and I have experienced them as well.

Yes I know that Thato my son. You see, if or when you are feeling sad, just take that very same feeling and feel it, be aware and realize the state of emotion you are engaged in this or that moment. All that I am saying is that, take a feeling that you are feeling now and feel it with the feeling that you are feeling. In other words, if you feel bad, take the bad feeling and feel it up with bad. Press that feeling by feeling it. How does it feel to feel sad?

Lol, now that is a funny question because when I feel sad I feel sad.

Exactly my point, you feel sad because you have not been feeling sad. If you were feeling sad you would not be feeling sad, you would however feel something different from sad.

No, no, no... I am so sorry I am against you on this one Thato, just simply because you are not making any sense.

Okay, I see you still do not understand. I tell you this, there is only one feeling, and that feeling is called feeling. There is only one emotion and that emotion is called emotion. You feel sad, happy, angry, bad, upset, jealous, petty, and all of the rest of emotions that you feel. Let us look at i carefully, let us observe it and let us realize it. What is anger? What is love? What is hate?

Lol, mmmhhhh... I see where you are going with this. Well love is a feeling anger is a feeling and hate is also a feeling.

Good, very good my son. So what would you call a feeling?

Lol, I would say a feeling is that which I am feeling now.

And what would it be that which you are feeling now?

Lol, I would or could be feeling love or any part of feeling.

Yes my son, yes my father, you are all good and good is all. So when you feel something, you are feeling it. The only thing that seems to be difficult is that, you may like or not like that which you are feeling at any moment, and also remember that to be like, you have to observe like and thus become like. You become that which you like. That which you like and are happy with, you say you love it, and that which you do not like and are no happy with you say that you hate it, it makes you sad, you are unpleased with it, and all of these are just feelings of feeling. Nothing is happening tc you but that which you are feeling, and all that you are feeling is just a feeling that which you have as many times have chosen to experience. So all that you are doing is to feel....

Can I put you to hold and we will discuss this when I come back from work and or school, I mean I would love not to go and just talk to you the whole day until I am tired of talking to you. But now I have to cut you short, because I have to do some extra for that which I am having difficulties with and understanding, and that is need. I have to go to work or school because I think I need that job or education to keep me floating. I know you have spoken to me in some clearer terms and understanding, but at this moment it still seems that I need to pay my rent Thato. So see you later hey!

Oka my man, I will hala at you.

Thank you Thato for listening, thank you for being here and there for me in this way.

You are all welcome Thato.

Hey, I am back. How are you doing?

I have been here waiting for you!

In other words I have been waiting on myself?

Yes you have indeed.

Okay, you were explaining about feeling before I left for work or school the other day.

Yes I was. Now listen again. All that you have to do is to feel. Feel your skin now and you will feel the smoothness or roughness on you of your skin, and that is it, it is just smooth or rough sometimes or at some parts.

Okay I hear you. Now tell me this, what if I feel like killing someone because they have made me upset and extremely angry, what if they have crossed that which I call my line boundary? What should I do, how should I react to such situation or circumstances?

I see, you still do not understand. The answer is so simple as all the time. I have just told you now, that all you have to do is to feel. You say that you feel like killing someone. Well I tell you this, if you kill that person it is an act, it is not a feeling, a feeling does not suggest for you to kill. A feeling is truly felt and not truly acted out. You can act to love someone or something in particular way, but that does not mean that you are feeling that, because you have put an act in place of what you are feeling. So now I tell you this, killing is an act. Some people will even kill for love, and if you ask a person why he or she did so? They will or would say, "because I loved that someone whether it is a she or he so much that I did not want to lose him or her so much to someone or something". Some people kill for fun, they feel happy after having someone killed, they get good blood rushes or chills from that. And some people kill for other various reasons they have thought of and or about whether may it be revenge or spitefulness and or for money. So you see that you can put or pull an act in order to feel a certain way. We can also say that actions trigger feelings and feelings trigger actions. You can, will and may feel extremely angry or

86

obnoxious at someone or something, but do realize that you are only feeling angry, and when you feel angry you start to create an entire existing thought being of imaginative memory. You start to think of things to do and not to feel, you think of an act that will justify your feeling according to you. So then, a person can feel angry and just cry about it, or just hit or bang on things. A person can feel anger and just go kill someone and say that they were feeling angry and upset because of one act that one other person pulled or did against them. So then my son, do not confuse your actions for what you are feeling, and do not confuse your feelings for what your actions outputs. It is just a feeling and not an action or an act, and it is just an act and not a feeling. All there is to be and do is to feel, oh yes feel yourself my son, feel your feelings, feel it and feel them.

Mmhhhh... woahh... man, you can talk hey! Just listening to you is very breath taking.
Now remember this. Your mother's actions have made you upset, angry, confused, sad, happy, glad and joyful. Your friends, girlfriends, teachers, lectures, colleagues, bosses and many other related to you closely have also made you feel the same way as your mother has. You have been feeling all the same parts of feelings towards and from those that you are related to, it has all been the same feelings of feeling, it is all one feeling, and that feeling is a feeling.
So what is that one feeling that I have been feeling?
Aaahhmmmm... tricky for you, but not me! You see I do not call it anything, but I know what you would call it. What would you call a feeling?
I do not know, that is why I am asking you. Would you call it Nothing?
Call it whatever you want to call it as you have so done now. And you still do not understand. A feeling is just a feeling my son.
So you are saying that if I feel in a particular way towards someone, it is the same to the other person?
Well yes, what did you expect? I tell you this, you love everyone the same, because you feel the same feelings towards everybody, anybody or anything. The anger, love, hate, joy and passion, you have thus felt all of these feelings towards anything you have encountered in your experiences, and remember that it has all just been feelings of feeling.

Yes… That is exactly what I was trying to explain and say when I told you that I do not judge and that I love all the same. The love I have for my mother, is the same love I have for my girlfriend and so forth…..

Lol, I know my son, I just wanted to explain more to you, so that you can make more sense of that which you were saying about you loving people all the same way. You are slowly waking up to realization that there is only a feeling.

Oh… so this is what I was trying to say? Man, bingo! Thanks Thato.

I tell you this, bad feels really good when you feel it, anger feels good when you feel it, love feels good when you feel it, and hate feels good when you feel it. I tell you this, the minute you realize that you hate someone, it is the minute you realize that you love them because you have been feeling them.

Okay, I do understand this feeling part now, I do get you.

Good, I am glad that you do. Now we can move on to our next big subject… and that is feeling.

But we just spoke about feelings now.

I know… you just type, listen and read.

Okay, let's do it, I am ready.

You do remember. You have remembered.

Yes I do remember.

Now I tell this, this is the scariest good part of these notes you have decided to take and embark on. This is almost all of it.

Lol, okay this sounds… ahhhhmmm how should I put it? Confusing and interesting.

Oh…. Yes it is, oh yes it is my son.

Now I tell you this. Language and words do not make sense. Language is all made up! Language is so confusing that if you were to really listen to it, if you really listen to what you are saying, you would laugh until whenever. You will realize the truth as you have realized it now. Me and you my son are going to analyze that which you call language, we will look into it very deep than you have throughout the years of your self-known existence.

Mmmmmmhhhh…. Now this seems and sounds very, very interesting. Please tell me all about it.

Yes I am my son, we are going to engage in a senseless meaningful dialog. And when we are done with being crazy, we will go through some more of all that you can imagine.

Now let us begin.
Do you know what is your name.
Yes I do know what is my name.
So then you do agree that what is your name?
What? What do you mean that what is my name? My name is not what. My name is Thato and not what.
You said that you do know that what is your name. So that means that what is your name. And now, let me get this, your name is Thato and not what?
Yes that is my name.
I thought you said Thato and not what is your name. And now you are saying that is your name. So what is your name actually? Is it that? What or Thato and not what?
Mmmmmm…. I need to know if you are asking a question or telling me what my name is.
Well how would you like to make of it?
I see where you are going with this, you are trying to change all that I know and all that I was taught by my parents and teachers or I should say elders.
Trust me my son, I am not trying anything, you are trying anything and everything. You wanted to know what is what? How is what? Why that is what? And I am doing exactly that, I am giving what you have given to yourself Thato my son. Do you now see that you can make anything of anything that you choose to be and confuse yourself just for the sake of it? Do you realize that you can make anything up as you choose to make it all up! And I promise you that you do not even know where is up.
I know where is up.
Yes, where is up.
Up is on top of me, it is above or over me.
Mmmmmmm… so if up is on top, it is above or over you, so it does not make it where.
No, no, no, so if it is not on top or above me, so where is it?

89

You see, there you go again, and yes I do agree that where is it, and it is where. I will make a simple famous say of all your now time. Have you ever heard of:

It is what it is?

Yes I have.

Then I tell you this, it is what it is, it is what you make of it, and what you make of it is that, and what is that and that is what. That is why you ask why, because why is that.

Lol, so let me get this right. Why is that.

Yes!

That is why.

Yes!

Where is what.

Yes!

What is that, and where is that.

Yes!

This is that.

Yes!

Where is everywhere.

Yes!

I am here.

Yes!

Here is where. And where is here.

Yes!

Lol, and we are here. And here we are.

Yes!

This is fun, and it actually makes sense.

What is fun?

Yes!

Ahhhhhh, you got it!

Thato is me, just as me is Thato?

Yes! Yes, and yes! You see, you made up words to can express what you are feeling, and what you are feeling is not your words. When you were birthed, you knew Nothing of words, terms and language as you now know them to be. All you did was to cry and laugh, and crying was the best uttered meaning to you when you were a baby. You see, a baby knows what it is feeling and how it is feeling it. When it is hungry it cries, when it feels sleepy it still cries, when it receives no attention it still cries, when it seeks an experience and does not meet it, it still cries. And when the experience is met, the baby smiles, giggles, or laughs all by itself. When the baby is entertained it laughs at the entertainment and the entertainer. So then, as you grew up, you decided to make sense of words from voices of sound, and that is to say, you made sense of and for sound There was and is no meaning for sound. Sound is sound or voice uttered and that is it. Sound is everywhere. Everywhere is Sound. So then, you took sound and adjusted it, you tuned voices of sound to be loud, soft, hard, weak, and strong frequencies and thus gave meaning to each of what you have made up and adjusted from sound of voice. After tuning and adjusting sound, you gave more meaning to each frequency of tuned sound. You decided to give descriptions of hard, soft weak, strong, low, and fast sound pitch. Each frequency tuned stood for a particular emotion and or expression.

Yes you have remembered.
I have remembered.
In your language, you have thus best put it. You say Nothing makes Sense. But you reject and refuse to say that sense makes Nothing, but that which you call words from voice do say and suggest that Nothing makes sense. Can you make sense of just one continuous single frequency wave of sound?
No I cannot, because it will just be noise of sound.
So do you agree that sound makes no sense?
Lol, yes I do agree.
Well I do promise you that, that is what you have done with sound, you have given it meaningless meanings, you even made music from sound to the noise variation levels of sound that you think is suitable and understandable to you. And I tell you this, you have made no sense at all, all that you have written down on these notes makes no sense because you have made it all up. You gave meaning to no meaning, and you have imagined in your memory sound with meaning and thus turned it to written words from sound. Have you heard of the language called slang? Well I tell you this, it is and was made up. Right now, you Thato my son, you speak that which you call Sotho. Well I tell you this, that language called Sotho is and was made up. Have you heard of a language called

Afrikaans? Well I tell you this, it was all made up. But where does all of this made up stuff come from, what was and is the first Language? I will still tell you this, you first language is your cry of thought, your first language is you laughter of thought, that is your first understanding of feelings, that is your first understanding of things.

Wait, wait, and you just wait! So are you saying that if I want to know what happened in the past of human history I should remember my past? Nope, I am not saying that, but you can imagine it and make it all up if you choose it to be so in that sense. You see, I am making sense of you coming to know language as it is now, and you are making sense of it in a sense of historical existence. Remember that the purpose of these notes is to know who Thato is. It is to know who you are! These notes are not about the other person, they are about you, and anything that is said and written down here can and will be held against you, because it is you.

Okay, so yah continue, you were talking about sound and language. And oh yah, just for the record, I have done and read life. I have read about the string theory, I have read and heard a little bit of the big bang theory, I have watched a video of fractals, and when I was growing up, I imagined myself and I saw myself being this great scientist in the world and working on big projects. And once I realized that I was and have been moving away from that which I imagined myself to be, I then considered being a musician. Mmmhhh, I remember it very well. I remember it well because I used to make records with my friends outside on windy and dusty days of the township I am from to make songs. We used cassette tapes to record, our instruments were simple tins and boards to create that which we thought was reasonable sound to produce a song with good instruments and lyrics. After that was not working out as I thought at that time of moment as a child, lol, I then realized that I could actually become a rapper. I should tell you this, rap music influenced most of my knowledgeable readings and studies of different material. Because I wanted to write meaningful songs, it actually pushed me to read more books just about everything that which I liked and loved. And in doing so, my vocabulary was expanding and thoughts broadened. Although I must admit that I have lost most of my vocab because I stopped reading, writing and rapping. And oh trust me I wrote good and bad lyrics, some were good, some were super good, and some were bad, but the lyrics were good in general. Some were bad because they had some of that which people consider as evil. I attended some few poetry classes here and there. I even took books to read at work, I used to write songs while I was at work... and through all of this, I had questions for days, I could not understand that which people believe and that which people imagine to be real or false. Me and my friends would talk, debate and argue about who God is, politics, and what is a woman and how to have sex with her, and how to make our lives better. hhhhaaaa.... I could go on for long with my past, so yah please tell me more about language.

Good, thank you for sharing. Did you just realize that you were remembering there? You never talk about your young past like this.
Yah, and it is good to pour my feelings of past like this.
So yah, I tell you this, there are many languages in the world, and of that many some are not recorded. How do you think European settlers communicated with South Africans when they first explored the cape? I tell you this, it was impossible to communicate. Force had to be applied for communication because there was no understanding. Trickery had to be done for communication's sake to establish an understanding. One way or the other, one party had to know and understand the other one's language. It did not matter which party knew what language, but communication had to be established efficiently between the merchant travelers of settlers from Europe and the people staying in the cape of Africa in South of Africa. If all people would come together and speak at the same time, you would hear Nothing but a loud noise of vibration like bees do buzz in variation.
Lol, so we are actually buzzing because we are all talking and communicating at the same time now in the world. Lol, wow this is good information. And if I was to listen to all the people now, I would actually hear Nothing but a buzz... wow, wait, wait, wait..... I would actually hear the buzz ringing in my ear. Now this reminds me to ask you about the buzz ringing in my ear, what is it all about hey?
Aaaaahhhhhh... Thato my son, you have answered yourself and you still ask for an answer. I tell you this, call it whatever you want to call it. You see, we are going back to what we said earlier about sound. Now you can hear a ringing sound in your ear and you want to know the cause of it, you want to label it, you want to call it something. You would like to know the meaning of that sound, and that is how it all started. That is how it all

begun. Wanting and choosing to know what that sound is, started a thing called language. It started a thing called a word from the voice of sound you are or were making. So then, I ask you now, what would you like to call it? What would you like to call that ringing sound in your ear?
Nope, I am not going to call it anything or answer that. I will not make things up just like that.
So then I tell you this, language is and was made up, language developed and evolved through time. When language was established, you realized that language does not make sense, in so, you then modified it. You developed grammar on how words of language should be said. You made statements into questions and questions into statements, and you placed commas, full stops, exclamations and so forth. You gave names to this idea and thought of tuning sound. In doing so you thus invented your grammar and rules of and to sound you were making, you named and called it vowels or consonants from the sound of voice you were making. Now then, because without regulatory rules to best suit sounds produced from mouth, that means whatever you say will make no sense at all, and therefore you thus made an understanding of what makes no sense at all indeed, and have made rules for it. You did this because you saw the no sense you were making or saying, you realized that language of words is one cord expression of feeling, and remember that a feeling is just a feeling. A cry does not have a meaning, and laughter does not have meaning as well. Someone can and may cry when happy or sad, and also someone can and may laugh when sad or happy..... And you feel all that which you feel.

I tell you this, have you seen the latest SMS phone text and or social media language? My friend, that language is so made up and you still understand it. You type, "lol", and you give it a meaning of Laughing Out Loud. And if a teenager does not understand that, you say that they are stupid and or are retarded. But if an old person of forty five does not understand, you say it is okay because it is a different language than of that they are used to and or have learned, and you understand this.
I tell you this I am not stupid when I choose not to know and understand English!
I am not stupid if I cannot read what you made up!
I am not stupid when I do not understand Math!

I am not stupid for failing to do things your way!
I am not stupid for failing to do your order!
I am not stupid for failing what you understand!
I am not stubborn for not doing what you want!
You are stubborn for not letting me do what I want!
I am failing your understanding because you fail to understand my understanding.
I can only pass what I understand. And I have to make up all that which I understand.

Now I tell you this.
In your time now, you have that which call sign language, it is a language said to be for the deaf. The deaf cannot hear what you say, but there are those who can lip read without having to use that which was meant for them as a language. Sign language is and was created and developed only to generalize an understanding for those who say and think that they can hear sound, and to those who say and think that they cannot hear sound. On top of all this, another need was and is spotted for those who could not see but can hear sound. Thus brail, was created for the blind. You see Thato my son, in order to can establish proper understanding and communication, there has to be an agreement, there has to be an understanding between those who have a common goal. You Thato my son, say that someone who is blind or deaf is sick. You say that they are not as they should be born, you think that there is only one form of experiencing being a human. You do not see the back of the mind, the mind chooses its experiences with the other mind it chooses as it knows itself to be. You see once you understand communicative relative love, a shared thought, once you understand imagination, once you understand that you are a memory, you will thank yourself as who you are.
I tell you this, all these languages were created, developed and made all up for some one form of particular understanding.

I will make another perfect example according to you and me.
Since you now know that I am you, and you are me, we will both realize this. I tell you this, math is and was created to reach one form of understanding. You see with math, you have been establishing and

refining that which you call the universe. In order to can define the universe, you wanted know the smallest things first. You wanted know how you move from point A to point B. you wanted know how long it takes you from that point to that point. In order for you to can do this, in order for you Thato to can do this, you had to put yourself in an imaginative world of math, you had to create numbers that which were never there. I tell you this, a number does not exist. You imagined it, and you thought it to be whatever it is. You made it all up just as you have done with your life and language. You developed a system for and of math. You convinced yourself that it exists, and you convinced others as well that it is the way you have realized it as you call it math of numbers in your thoughts of imaginative memory.

Come, let us test each other and see if we are still mathematicians.

Okay, let us do it.

Let us try this.

What is 1 + 1?

Lol, lol, that is just so kindergarten, it is so lame that I do not have to answer it.

Oh no, please, I would love for you to answer it.

Okay, for your pleasure, I will then.

1 + 1 = 2. You see, that is and was very easy, I did not even have to think hard about it man.

Lol, and now I tell you this. 1 + 1 = 1.

Nah, hell no, you get out of here. How can one number plus the other one number be one?

Well, it is because you are adding one number to another one number, if there is only one number, where do you get the other one from? There is no any other number but that one number, and that one number is this number, and also this and that number are this number, and that is it. You can even take one 1 and put it on top of the other one 1, it will always be one. But because you choose it to be an understanding that you want, then so it is as you think and believe it. I tell you this, there is only one number, and that number is that 1.

You cannot take one number and add it to one number. If it is so, where does the other one come from? I tell you this, you have and had to imagine that there is another one like this or that one.

Lol, okay. Now that is interesting to know.

Yeah, I told you that it was going to be interesting and scary at the same time at this point.
Yah you did hey.

You now, on this imaginative space of place you have placed yourself through thought that you are, have different measuring system, you have the metric system and the imperial system. Some people understand the other one over the other. You see, I could go on with this, but right now, I am defining who you are Thato. I am with you because I am now, right here now you. You have asked me your main question, and that is and was that do you really need to need? And I tell you this, I will give answers to you on these notes, right here on this paper, book or device that you are holding now my son.
Okay, I hear you.
So yah, whatever you agree to, you will have understood it by choosing it the way it is as you think it to be. So far you have agreed on all the things you have been taught by the older you. I have directed your life, I told you all that you know now since from your birth of thought. And I changed my mind of what I have known myself to be.

I tell you this, listen to the sound of the earth.
Listen to the sound of birds.
Listen to the sound of insects.
Listen to the sound of people.
Listen to the sound of rain.
Listen to the sound of sound.
Oh my son, listen to the universe, hear it call up on you. Listen and you shall hear. Hear it, and you shall listen to it.
Speak to what you are listening. Flow to what you are listening.
Be rhythmically one with the vibration of happiness, love and joy. Tune to this feeling and vibrate to it.
There is glory in thy sound.
There is peace, and there is you.
And you are it. And that is why I love you.

Oh me, I have remembered.
Yes you have remembered.

Now I want you to read this, look at it, in fact write it, you can even listen to it if you want and then read it, and this is your truth.

Have you ever wondered where the light leads to?

Okay, that's new. What do you mean now? Which light are you talking about?

Lol, hhaaammm..... I am talking about the light that you know, the one that you have always known, the one that you have always used and played with.

Are you talking about the sun?

Well is that the only light that you know?

Well technically yes, but that's not the only one that I know. I know electrically produced light, radiant and reflective light as well.

Good, very good my son, I am glad that you are remembering all of this.

What, you mean that you did not know?

Nope, I did but we are remembering here. Remember? And so you are remembering. Now then, I tell you this, light is darkness and darkness is light. This simply means that, that which is light is darkness and that which is darkness is light. Please let me finish, do not interrupt me here by asking me what I am actually trying to explain. So keep your question and listen, and I will give to you the pleasure of an answer.

Oh no please go on. Lol, how did you know that?

See what I mean? I am you man. Anyways, as I was saying before I got interrupted rudely by me, lol. Here is an untold story of your time, you have believed and you still do believe that you can see only where there is light. You believe that you need light to can see things or otherwise you will not be able to see things, you will not be able to differentiate what is what and which is what without light. And also you have believed and yes you still do believe that you cannot see in the dark. You believe that you do not need darkness to can see things or otherwise you will not be able to distinguish what is what and which is what in the dark.

And you know what? All this is good and good is all. Now I am going to tell you something interesting, something that will stretch your mind more than you have to at this point you are now at. Now I tell you this, and you have to be attentive, and always know that you are not forced to listen or to be attentive. You cannot see in the dark and in fact you will never see a thing in complete dark. This you know very well, this you have no problem with, I mean it is your believe after all and you have thus concluded. Now I tell you this, you cannot see in the light and in fact you will never see a thing in complete light. You see, if there was only light out there, you would see Nothing except for that light, there would be Nothing but light. So then such a question as this would arise, but what am I really seeing here, what am I looking at? And the answer would be Nothing, Nothing at all. You see, if there was only darkness out there, you would see Nothing except the dark, there would be Nothing at all but dark. So then such a question as this would arise, but what am I really seeing here, what am I looking at? And the answer would be Nothing, Nothing at all. You would be looking at something and you would not tell what it is, it would be just that, and I mean exactly that. So what exactly do we have here? Another question would arise.

I tell you this, in order for you to can be able to see, you needed both. You needed the light and the dark. After you had remembered and realized this, you then could see the light. Oh my… how amazing this was and still is for you, how beautiful it is to can see the light, how beautiful it is to can see the dark, it is indeed amazing and beautiful to see this because without any of them I cannot see a thing. Would you?
Lol, I do not think so.
How would you think it then?
Lol, again I would think it so.
So as we have said it, we need both to can see. Lightness or and darkness can be adjusted just as sound and this you also know it to be true. But wait a minute here, you just wait buddy. Now look at this, how can you adjust light in lightness, how could and can you adjust dark in darkness? Now this you never thought of. Wow what magnificent discovery it is for you, we should actually say what a remembrance this is to you. Now I tell you this, follow that which you call light my son, follow it. Light will take you to everything that is and was never there, light will reveal to you what is not.
Okay, so which or what light are you talking about?
I am talking about the light that you see, the light darkness and or the darkness light. You see light in the dark, and you see dark in the light, however you cannot see light in light and or dark in dark. I am talking about the light that is always there, and this is the light dark, and or dark light! I am and will show you how to follow the stars, how to walk on the

sun, how to jump from one planet to another. I will show you the life that you have always desired, the life that you have dreamt about, the life that you created in your dreams of thought being of imaginative memory.

No... no... no... now that sounds like a fantasy!

Yes indeed it is, you are living your fantasy right now, you are living your dream now my son.

We will make it all up just as Language is and was made up.

We will be the greatest of me and you that there ever was.

We will be legends!

Now I tell you this.

The greatest thing of things is understanding. Understanding is the greatest of all the made up nonsense we have written so far. You see once you understand that there is no language, there is no suffering, there is no wealth, there are no riches, there is no poverty, there is no pain, there is no hurt, there is no love, there is no hate and that there is only Nothing out there, you will have understood. Oh my son, my understanding has brought me bliss and it has brought wonders to others. Some have been hurt because of my understanding, and some have been blessed through my understanding. Understanding confused me a lot when I was where you are now.

Wait, so where are you now?

Ahhhhrrrggg.... I am everywhere I thought myself to be, and now I think myself to be where you are. Remember we are here? And here we are.

Lol, yes I do.

You see.... You are confused already, you do not even know what I am talking about and you do not even know what you are talking about. You see when I was where you are, I chose to see things differently than I was when I was not where you are...

I do not understand what you are talking about, and in fact I do not know it.

Yah it is okay, because I understand Thato my good friend. Now I tell you this, if you understand now that everything is perfect, and that everything is good, you will see. Once you understand that all that there is, is all made up, you will laugh at your understanding. A person who understands does not ask questions. Why would you ask about that which you understand! When a person asks why, that means they do not understand the cause of one particular word said or action done. To you it might seem too difficult, because there is and are way too much many things to can understand.... You see a question is posed to gain understanding of things, you cannot ask that which you already know of. Once you understand you shall not even ask why your girl cheated on you. Once you understand you will not be mad, angry, heartbroken or upset at someone for refusing to be with you or fall in love with you the way you would expect them to. Once you understand you shall not ask why did your mother die, because you already know now that she will pass on, and also once you understand you will not ask why am I born a cripple or disabled as you have chosen to label it and make it up. Once you understand you shall not laugh at someone who cannot speak English because they have chosen for it not to be their language through their thought of imaginative memory. Oh my son, once you understand you will even realize why you did not give that poor old beggar some few coins of money, once you understand you will realize why you killed and murdered that young boy, son, family, daughter, father, mother, sister and yourself. And the craziest part is when you realize that you have been understanding all this time, you will then understand that you have been understanding.

Okay I hear you. So you are saying that when I see a crazy person I should understand that he or she is crazy?
Nope, what I am saying is that you are crazy! Even that which you call a crazy person knows that you are crazy because you do not understand. That is why in most cases you find that which you call crazy people minding their own and doing their own things in their own ways because they know that you think they are crazy. And here is the craziest part again, you hardly and rarely barely ever hear a crazy person asking questions, they do not ask because they understand you as you are, and they understand themselves as they are. They know why you do the things you are doing now. Heck that which you call a crazy person never worries about wealth, fashion and luxury, in fact they think that all of that is crazy. But because they know why all of that is happening, it really does not matter. A crazy person is rarely barely ever worried, but you worry about them, my man you are crazy to think that someone can be crazy. You see, a crazy person knows and understands things, that is why they rather laugh at it because they know what is going to happen next and

what is really going on here, that is why they laugh all the time because it is all just funny. And you my son are becoming crazy every moment because you are asking question and having asked them, you receive answers from your daily moments of experiences and thus you write them down here because you understand and have remembered.

Come let us share a life experience.
When you are in a train, bus, taxi or an airplane and one or two of your life's funny moments of your memory come to your mind and you want to laugh…. On that you realize that you are in a taxi and there are people around you, and you hold your laughter because you know what people would think of you. You know that they would think that you are crazy when you just start laughing out of the blue, and if you were to laugh, someone next or opposite to you would stare at you in an ugly manner or ask you what you are laughing at? And if you were to respond you would say something like… "ah… Nothing.", or, " Just thinking of the past." But because you know what the other person is thinking and you are the one who is thinking it, and you think that he or she will think that you are crazy. And also if you do just burst into laughter, your thoughts will be true, and your thoughts were or are that people will think you are crazy and when you turn around and look at them on their faces after laughing you will realize that… oh my God they really do think that I am crazy. The more you realize it, the more funnier it gets, and the more funnier it gets you then realize that you have been thinking and Nothing has happened but a lot has happened in your thoughts because you were thinking of what the next person is thinking. Once the other next person thinks that you are crazy, he or she will be crazy because that person will be thinking that you are crazy and you are also thinking that you are crazy, in fact you will both be thinking about crazy. So you rather not laugh in a taxi, train, bus and or an airplane, but you rather internalize it or just smile at it. But you do not realize that by not explaining laughing your thoughts out is crazy too. By not sharing your thoughts with random people is crazy… yes it is crazy because you understand, and when you understand you just let things be. So yes you are crazy as hell my boy. All of you is crazy my son, and I mean everywhere you have been and everywhere you are, is crazy my son.

Lol, now that was funny.

Yes, I know, and everything will be funny once you understand. You will even laugh at funerals.

Lol, why would I do that?

You see, because you do not understand, you have thus asked why? I will tell you this to remind you, remember that you are dreaming all the time. You are moving in and out of thought being of dreams of imaginative memory in all moment of time, so yes, you will not die, you shall never ever die. And I know you do not understand now, but I will give to you explanations of all of this and you will understand after.

Okay, I am ready. And if I understand all of this I will be crazy?

Yep.

So this means you are crazy?

If you see me that way, then yes. Remember that you are talking to yourself here, you are talking to you, you are thinking to you, you are writing to you, this is a letter posted to you from you by you. You are doing this to or for no one else but you.

Okay I get it. Continue please.

That which you call a dead person is sleeping...

Sorry, I just remembered something from the bible here. I remember the story of Lazarus and Jesus... I remember that it was written that Jesus said to the dead corpse of Lazarus to come out!

Yes it is and was written so.

Well is it true?

I tell you this, what do you think?

I think so.

You see, you cannot think of what you are not thinking.

Okay what do you mean?

I mean that in order for you to think of it to be true, for obvious reasons you thought about it being not true. You see, you cannot differentiate that which is one thing. Remember that, that is that and it is what it is, and that is it. And if all is one thing, there cannot be the other, in order to can differentiate Thato, you need Ronald, Alfred, Thabiso, Kgaku, Tebello, Mokete or J.C, Andrei Damane or Rudi, you need the other person to can know who Thato is. If there is only Thato, then there is no other.

So if you think that Lazarus woke from the dead, it is because you thought he was dead, and that is that and that is it, and it is that.

Mmmhhhhhhh... I see what you mean, and I understand you Thato. So you are saying that Lazarus could be dead or awaken to life depending on what or how I think of it?
Yes indeed that is what you are saying.
Okay then good.

So then, I tell you this. A person can sleep as long as they choose to sleep...
Oh wow, and if they sleep now instantly for a long time and I mean like for seventy years or so, I will think that they are dead?
Yes indeed that is what you will be thinking if you think it so. You should ask yourself what that dead person is thinking right now, you should think of where he or she went and you will see that you might just follow them on the spot.
Oh wow, is this one of the reasons why some people die at funerals?
I tell you this, what do you think?
Oh.... I .... I think so.
Then good!
Lol, this is sad, and it is all funny at the same time, I do now see what you meant that I will laugh at funerals because I will have an understanding. And all of this seems and sounds so crazy!
Tell me about it, I know hey. People can sleep, some sleep in coma for one, two or three years, and when that person wakes up, you call it a miracle. Which indeed is exactly that. That person's dream was to perform a miracle from a long coma and he or she did exactly that. You also find people who can meditate for a month, and that is not so much different from a person who is in a coma, the only difference is that a person in coma does not sense or feel but can still hear and breathe. And a person who does deep meditation wishes to leave the body while it is still inhaling breath, seeing, hearing and feeling. A person who is in a coma also experiences deep meditation, that is why when they wake up they come back as changed persons and less fearful of death. That which you call a dead person or body wishes and wills to have Nothing to do with the flesh, the body can be left where ever and whenever the person feels that this is it and I am enough of this. The body can be dropped or left in the road... and this is what you call an accident... a person can jump from a

building and this you would call suicide... and a person can start a fight only to experience to be shot or stabbed to death sleep by thought.

Wait, so you mean that all deaths are suicidal?

I tell you this, what do you think? You see, this is the thing you call understanding. I understand how and why things are happening and thus I am not asking questions but mostly supplying you with answers. Once you understand this, there will be more questions on that and this. The ones which you understand, you will not even entertain them.... Now that you understand this few lot, you wait and see what is coming for you... oh you will love it and hate it my son. So I tell you this, people sleep my son and in their sleep, they dream and experience the things that you have imagined. This is one of the reasons why babies sleep a lot. In order for you to practice this sleep routine, you will have to be a baby all over again Babies know how to sleep, in fact they struggle with waking up, babies and small children are annoyed by being awake. You should see all the smiles and joys on a sleeping baby. They even giggle in their sleep, and this is all because they are experiencing joy and total bliss in a different place they imagine themselves to be while maintaining their baby bodies that belong to a particular parent all at the same time. A baby can and could be imagining itself to be an adult, and the fact that in the imagination of the adult version of the baby, the baby thinks itself to be a baby, it actually knows that somewhere it is a baby and also that somewhere it is an adult, and then it laughs at it all.... You as an adult you will be like," oh that is so cute and adorable, oh how sweet is this baby, oh it looks so cute." Oh well then finally the baby grows and becomes a confused teen and adult, it experiences its thoughts. It struggles and does not understand its creation of imaginative memory, it starts to question why and how is all the bad things happening to it, it experiences poverty, riches, lack or need, hunger, pain, love and all that it knows from thought being of imaginative memory. It adapts to what it is taught and forgets of how cute and adorable it was in its imaginative memory.

Aahhhhhhh... then finally the baby becomes old and realizes that it is and was cute again. This is one of the reasons why old aged people sleep a lot and do Nothing just as babies do. It is so because they are no different from babies and they have realized that there is Nothing to do. After realizing that all it did was for Nothing, the baby goes to sleep for as long as it chooses itself to be at old age, and that my friend you would still call it death. So yes then, old should learn from the young, and the young should learn from the old. In my own words I would say, the old should remember the young and the young should remember the old. Hhhhhhmmm... this is all good news to me, but it feels so crazy and insane at the same time.

Nothing wrong with being crazy, we spoke about this remember?

Yes I do.

So then, for you to be rich and have that which whatever you call riches, just sleep over it and you will wake up to it. Just use your imagination, I tell you this, sleep my son, sleep and wake up to riches, wake up now and you will be rich. Realize where you wish and would like to be, and then after, will all that you wish, like and want. And once you can will your sleep, you will, will your wake state. You will see no need for struggle, you will see no need for hunger, you will see no need for food the moment you realize no need. Stop realizing need and realize no need.

Now come closer... I am going tell you how and when to wake and why you are waking up to what you now know yourself to be.

Remember that there is a shared thought. A shared thought you experience it with and for others for yourself. Someone is dreaming about other people struggling and experiencing pains and suffering, and you are involved in the fulfillment of that dream. You have agreed to make it all possible, you have agreed to differentiate between poor and rich... so we need to get rid of that person, and put someone who can dream of riches and wealth for everyone and everybody.

Okay so in whose dream am I in now? And who is this person you are talking about?

That person is you my son.

Wait, wait, you just wait my man.... I do not wish for people to struggle, suffer and feel pain oaky! I wish for people to be rich and the best they are.

Okay, let me ask you this. Have you ever met a poor person?

Yes I have, I have seen plenty poor people on the streets.

You see what I mean? I have just told you that no one is struggling, no one is suffering or poor and no one is dying, and that all they are doing is dreaming of who and what they choose to be. But you still say that they

are poor because you think they were and are poor, and this you were thus told and taught. No one is rich, no one is poor, remember that I told you that words are just made up, they are labels placed for an experience of feeling. Nothing is happening to anybody, they are only experiencing a feeling, and they are feeling exactly how they see themselves to be.
Okay, but I was taught and told of the poor and rich, even Jesus knew of the poor and rich.
Remember that this is not about Jesus, this is about you! You said that you wanted to know who you are and what makes you as you are and why this form of state you now know yourself to be. Yes you were taught that from your young age, but you do not have to believe that it exists the way you have been taught. Remember that a baby knows Nothing of what you know now and a baby knows all that you know now in its imagination. An old person knows what a baby knows, and a baby know what an old person knows. I know what you know from your imagination, and you know what I know from my imagination of my memory.

A baby knows Nothing of riches, a child knows Nothing of riches. All that a baby wants and wishes to do is to have fun, all that a child does is to play and sleep, and it is all fun. That which you call a crazy person is not concerned about working, a crazy person just wants to be that which he or she is. That is why you find that which you call crazy people playing around and doing Nothing, they have no problem with it because they know and understand what you do not understand. It is also pointless for crazy person to can explain all of this because they already know that you are going to say that they are crazy. That is why they do not say much, and even when they do say something, it does not make sense to you, and they know all of this. They know that it is all made up, they also know that you are not making sense, but the fact that you think you are making sense, it is even funnier as hell because they also think that they are making sense. So a crazy person would rather laugh at you and just leave you be, it is so because you simply do not understand. You do not understand! You do not understand! And now all of this is written down here, you understand how it is. You might think that crazy people do not feel how you are feeling, oh trust me they do. But they also know that there is no need to cry over the dead, there is no need to feel sorry for the poor, they know that all of it is just a feeling of feeling thought being of imaginative memory.

Okay, I hear you.

I understand all that which you are telling me now. But now if you say that when we are in our deep sleep, we die here now, that means that everybody who is sleeping now is dead, that means there are a whole lot of bodies lying around everywhere, every day and every time one sleeps. Remember that I said, you will never die, you just simply wake and sleep into and from different realities as you have chosen them to be. And in sense you would be right in saying that, because if all bodies just slept where they are at that or this moment of instant, this means that people would sleep on the streets, work, school, planes, cars, houses, in water, on ships and just about everywhere, and in fact that is what is happening, people do sleep everywhere when they choose to in the now time of day, but you do not see it because you have divided a day by placing sunlight in a day as not to see one day but rather two of that very same one day. Many most of you, love the bodies you are in now, you love them so much that every time you choose to leave your bodies in safe places, and these safe places you call them homes. And when you sleep, you make sure it is safe on bed and out of harm's way so that you may return to them when you choose to use them again, unless you choose not to use them anymore you will remain to that side which you are in, only if there is no need of this body on this side. You do this because you know if you sleep while driving you will cause a definite horrible car collision accident on the road, you also know that if you leave your body or sleep while crossing the road you will get hit by cars and thus sleep forever this side and be awake where you choose to be.

Now remember this.

Remember how to see.

Remember how to look.

Your mirror is your eyes.

There is truth in the eyes, and all of everything that you can find is in the eyes.

And these are your eyes. And these eyes are yours.

The eye is the seer of all things.

You see all things that you have and are seeing. You are the seer.

One of many most things that you dislike is to be looked at, at anyhow you do not like. You know that your truth lies in your eyes, and this is to say that many pieces of you know that the eyes hold your true identity. If you look at me for just five seconds, ten, or even one minute you will see and know me, you will find out who I am through my eyes, you will see what I am thinking just by looking at my eyes, and after thinking of what I am thinking you will know what I am thinking because what you are thinking is what I am thinking.

Now listen to this, I will make a perfect example according to me and you that agrees with me.

When you are in the club, church, restaurant, office meeting or any other place that you can think of yourself being in, and you are in the company of people around you. If and or when you look at a hot lady or girl in miniskirts, and she turns and finds you looking at her in her mini skirt, that lady, girl, or woman will know that you are looking at her because she looked at your eyes and saw that you were looking at her, and what you are looking at is that she is wearing a hot sexy short skirt. Now that she knows that you are looking at her, she will think that you want to do her right sexually. She knows this because it is what you are thinking, you think that she is hot and sexy, and the only way for her to know what the other person is thinking, it is to look and stare them right in their eyes. And once she thinks that you want to do and give her sexual pleasures... you will also think what she is thinking. You will say in your thoughts that the girl, lady or woman thinks that you want her, and she will also think that you want her too. So now since you are thinking what she is thinking, and she is thinking what you are thinking, why do you not just do what you are both thinking? Because she thinks that you want her and you also think that you want her because she is wearing a short skirt with a sexy body... might as well let your thoughts come true.

Remember that understanding is crazy.
Understanding is wisdom.

Come. Here is another example.
When you see a poor person begging for money, you are afraid or you do not want to look at them in their eyes. You do this because you know that once you look and stare at each other's eyes one of you will think

something, and once one thinks something, you will also know and you already know what the next person is thinking because you are the one who is thinking about it. So when you look at the poor beggar in the eyes... the only way for him to know what you are thinking is to look right back at you. And once he or she looks right back at you, he or she will think that you feel petty for him or her. He or she knows this because you are feeling petty, he or she knows this because they can see all of it that which is in your eyes, and your eyes are full of petty, sorry and shame for him or her. You see this is all very crazy. You often ask yourself why is that or this person looking at me like this, like that or this way? But you never realize that the only way to can see that someone is looking at you, it is because you looked at them, it is to look right back at them... and if you truly observe right into their eyes, you will see and know what they are thinking and you will not even ask the question why because you will know and understand. I tell you this, every single person that you came across saw you, even those whom you think you never saw but you were there with. They saw you, because you saw them and you were exactly where they were!

Remember that this is all crazy.
And it is understandable.

I will give another example.
In your life now, you have couples, young and old who do not talk or speak a lot when in their company as a couple. Come, Listen!
You sometimes find that old couples in their sixties or seventies do not talk to each other that much, and when this is so, it is not just simply because they know each other, it is because they understand the communication of thought through the eyes. They know that whatever they want and choose to say, can be seen and looked at through the eyes, even if it is a lie. That is why you find couples who have been together for a very long time just always sit and smile at each other because they can see all the love the other one has for the other. And all you can do is just to smile at each other. But to you who does not know or understand this, you would think that they are a boring couple, and because you think it so, you shall see boredom, but they will be seeing joy, love and happiness together. I tell you this, if you really want to see why that couple is always

smiling at each other and never say anything much to each other, the three of you will have to sit down and look at each other right in the eyes of each other, and you will see what they have always been seeing, you will all see it and laugh at it.

So, if you choose and want to see something, just look at it. Remember that when you look at someone in the eye, when you look right into their eyes you will see yourself, you see a reflection of yourself. Since you see a reflection of yourself, you will realize that you are seeing your thoughts. That is how you see and know what someone else is thinking, you see this because you are reflecting your thoughts to them and them to you.
This is why you do not want to be looked or stared at for a short or a long time. When someone looks at you, you ask them or yourself of what they are looking at, you get annoyed and irritated by being looked or stared at. Heck you even get paranoid and suspicious of almost everything when someone looks at you. A person may be looking at your legs, but you would think for them that they may be looking at your thighs, or maybe your heels or new sneakers, you would even suspect that he or she thinks you have long legs, short legs, big fat legs, maybe because I am a crippled handicap and I walk funny, and now he or she is looking at me, oh... wait maybe he or she can see the scar on my leg, or burns. So does it really matter if someone sees that which you have and are and also see?! And guess what? The only way you can see that a person is looking at your legs, it is to look at their eyes, since you see their eyes, their eyes will tell and reveal to you what they are looking at and see, hence you will look at what they, he or she is looking at. You will see what they are looking at and that is how you notice that someone is looking at your legs. Even in your knowledge of knowing that a person is looking at your legs, you still have the guts and the nerve to ask what that person is looking at.
Lol.
Aha, you think it's funny, keep on laughing my friend.
But it is funny.
I know right?
Lol, okay, please continue.
People do not like being looked at. You do not like to be looked at for a while period. When someone looks at you, you even go to an extent of thought that they are looking at you because you are white, because you

are black, because you are coloured, because you are Chinese, African, European, Asian, American and so forth. You think so many things of what that person is thinking just by looking at their eyes, just by looking at their eyes you make all sorts of things up on assumptions. And shame poorly, the only way you can make it stop is to stop looking at what that person is looking at. Stop looking in to their eyes.

I tell you this, if you really want to know what that person is seeing, you should walk to them and look into their eyes. When you look straight into someone's eyes, you will see how beautiful that person is, you will see how beautiful you are since you will be reflected. You will see how much that person loves you, you will even realize that you love that stranger, and or that person. You both will see how you belong together, you will see all the pains, the bad, the good and struggles that person has been through, you will see them because they are yours, and that it is your reflection. You will even shed a tear for that person, and when you cry, that person will cry with you, because he or she sees what you are seeing in his or her knowledge. You will even smile because you both realized that it has turned out okay, it has all been good and good has it been all. And after that you can just laugh at it because it is all funny. You will see the no point of what you are seeing because you know what you are seeing, and by this time, you will then look away from that person. And this is how and why you keep on looking at every next person shortly and brief because you do not want them to see what you are thinking. And also this is why you would say that you do not want a person to look into your soul through your eyes. And the best way to do this is to look away every time any random person looks at you, you rather look at a person for a brief two seconds, five second and just maybe more. Because if you were to look at anybody for a while you will think and see what he or she is thinking and it will all start over again and again and this is all tiring for you. And this is what I meant when I said you are a prophet, you are a prophet because you can see everything that you choose and want to see!

I tell you this, you have remembered.
You do remember.
And now remember how to breathe. Remember that I said to you that you should eat breath? Now listen.

I tell you this, once you remember how to breathe as once as you were when you were a child, you will have remembered how and when to sleep, and you will remember what and when to sleep. And also once you remember how and when to sleep and to breathe as once as you were old as you can remember, you will have remembered how to sleep. Right now the control and understanding of breath taking, and that is to say inhalation or breathing in air is still misunderstood and done by you. You remember how to breathe and forget how to breathe. You see, a baby breathes in less air than an older baby does, and this is to say an adult older than any baby. You know that you breathe in more air than a child does because you see them small, you see them as small little things because you think you are older and bigger than you are when you were that small.

I tell you this.
The best way to fall in and out of deep dream state is to remember how to breathe, when you remember that breathing slow makes you more sleepier, and when you remember that breathing slow makes you unconscious from what you are conscious of, you will have remembered. You see, a baby sleeps a lot because he or she or it knows and has have remembered how to breathe. When you breathe slow or little air in, only so much little oxygen goes in to your body, and when there is little oxygen in your lungs of body, your heart slows down, and when your heart slows down it thus slows down the bodily operations. And when the bodily operations slow down, you use the lightest movement that you have always known how to use, and that is thought being of imaginative memory. Since your body is at rest, since your body has slowed down from movement, the only thing you can do is to imagine and think of all that you can do and be, and the more you think of what to do and be, the more you will do of what you are thinking. So in general you fall into your thoughts when you slow down one form of thought being. So then my child, I tell you this, you say you want to be rich, then fall into your thoughts of riches through sleep and waking to it by breathing.
Okay I hear you, but then that means if I slow down this form of thought being and not use it, because I do not like it, I will actually be killing what I am now.
Yes and no.

Yes kill that which you do not want to be, stop thinking about that which you are not, and the only way to do this is to take breath from that which you are now and blow breath into that which you choose, wish and want to be. No because you will be giving life to the rich version of that rich thought being itself to be. I tell you this, once you remember how to give breath to the rich version of thought being, you will not need that which you think you are now because you will have seen the no need of that which you do not like. You will leave this body right here and right now on this spot of instant of thought being imaginative memory. I tell you this, go ahead my son, go ahead my daughter, give life to the rich you want and choose to be. I tell you this, breathe life to the life you choose to have. You see, after having realized that you can give breath to anything you choose, after remembering how to breathe breath to that which you want to bring to life to, you will realize that there is no need to breathe life into that which you do not like yourself as or to. And when this happens, you say, "I am dead." You say this because you can see your thought lying there on the bed, chair, road, floor, in water or grave, and what actually happens is that you move away from that thought of sleeping on the bed, chair, road, floor, in water or grave and move on to the next place of thought you choose to be, and if you leave that thought there for a long period of sixty if not more years, those around you will think of you dead, and since they think you are dead you will be buried or they can even pull the plug off you as you have wished and thought it to be in your imagination. Then after, when you remember and realize that you have been buried for sixty years, you forget about that thought of you being buried because you do not wish to die, all that you want to do is to live right here now as you are addicted to life! And when you forget about your buried dead body, you choose to remember the last state of the very same body when it was on the bed before you forgot about it sixty years ago. And this is why you wake up in the morning and go to church, work, school, partying and or gym and say that you had a bad or horrible nightmare to a friend because you remembered that which you wanted to do with this body rather than that which has or had or will occur when you choose it to be. Once you remember this and understand this, you will not petty it, because you know it is just a thought. Since you know it is just a thought, you will willingly forget about that thought, and those around will think that you are dead, but you will know that you are not dead, hence you will not even worry. And once you forget what you know yourself to be, you will remember that which you choose to remember m son. You do this because you now know and understand that you can go back to it when you choose it by thought of remembrance.

Wow, wow, and wow some more... so this means that I die every moment, this means that every time I take a breath I give life to something else, this means that every second, mini and semi mini second of this instant moment I am killing a thought by forgetting it, I am killing a thought by changing my mind of how and who I am. And the only way to bring my thought back to life is to breathe into it and when I breathe into it I will see it, and after seeing it I will remember it. Depending on which o what state I remember myself to be, I therefore will return to that I am as I think myself to be... so, I can or could be in a car accident, I can or could be drowning, I can or could be sleeping, I can or could be in a coma, I can or could be killed by my mother by abortion, I can or could be crazy because I understand... And all of these things I am choosing them. Like for example as you have said earlier, the only reason I am cautious when I cross the road is that because I can see what will happen when I cross the road and that is to say that I will know what will happen when I cross the road, and what I know is that when there is a car approaching at some speed rate, I calculate and measure. This means that I foresee what will happen or I create what will happen in my imaginative memory, and what will happen is that when I cross the road and a car is exactly where I am at that moment of instant time, it will hit, knock and or kill me. And because I saw already what happened, I choose not to re-experience what has happened already because I saw that injured thought, I saw that dead thought, I saw that drowning me, I saw being raped, I saw being gay and having sex with men, I saw being lesbian and having sex with women, I saw and know what will happen if and when I jump off a building..... So you know what? I will not be or do that which I know will kill me, and the only way of doing this is to forget what I saw and not re-experience it again and again by thought as I have imagined it to creation, but then again I keep on doing what I do not want to experience because I cross roads every time, and every time I see and observe and know of what will happen when I cross the road now, and since I know of what will happen, cross roads spontaneously because I have done it many times and by

115

doing this, I will leave my thoughts where they are and whoever is there around that thought will see me or think of me dead. Because I know that I am not dead, so it really does not matter. Oh.... Oh my good God, oh my good lord, my goodness, oh goodness me! Lol, so you were right all this time when you said that I am old, you were right when you said I am old the way I know myself to be old!

Exactly!!! Exactly, and exactly my point!
Lol, Now you have remembered! This is what is called understanding, and this is understanding at its best. There are many of you who understand this. Understanding is bliss, and to those who do choose not to understand, it can be very awful and confusing for you and them because they do not understand what you have understood. Now that you understand so much little, I will answer your thoughts that you wanted to ask, I will answer what you have been thinking to ask yourself. You want to know why you yawn and or sigh. I tell you this, when you yawn you are not just simply tired. You yawn because you want to breathe breath into another life, you want to give life to another life of thought of imaginative memory you think you are. And when this happens, you say that you are tired, you say this because you are indeed tired of suffering the way you have conceived yourself to be by thought of imaginative memory in or on this side. The only way to cannot suffer is to find peace, and there only place full of peace is sleep. And once you sleep you go to your peace and your peace is your happiness and joy, and joy is all of that which you call riches and can does make you happy. When you sleep you then wake up to the side of riches and bliss, and once you realize that but this means that you are not sleeping, all that you are doing is just waking up to your own realized truth, you wake up to your own reality, and while all this is happening you are still sleeping. While still sleeping you are breathing the sweet breath of life to both lives from life! And also this is one of the reasons why you always sigh. You do this because you do not understand why you have to suffer so much for Nothing... and if your sigh is loud enough, someone may ask you of what is the matter? And you will try to explain your hustles, struggles, sufferings, pains and joys of pains.
I tell you this.
Go ahead and keep breathing because you will never stop breathing. Breathe to trees.

Breathe to animals.
Breathe to Earth.
Oh…. Breathe the breath of the universe!
And finally breathe life!
Let us raise a glass to life.
Let us raise ourselves to happiness.
Cheers to life living now and forever more now and then!
You are the sweet breath of Life.
I tell you this, every time you yawn or sigh, just remember that you do not like where you are at this and or that moment. Just remember that you want to be something else than that which you are now, just remember that you chose this, and that but you do not feel it anymore now as you did before now.

Now you have remembered.
Now you understand my son, my one and only son. Now you understand my daughter, my one and only daughter. Now I can add all that I have said to this one thing, now I can bring one home to itself and thyself. You see, now you know and understand how to breathe, see, and sleep, I will now close this form of understand you have enquired about, I will close this lack of understanding of thy oneself in this form thy one know itself to be my son. You see what still confuses you with that which you call dreams, and is in fact a short realization, is that you spend a little period in them. When you sleep, you sleep for… let us say minimum 4 hours, and maximum eight hours. In that four or eight hours there are breaks between deep sleep, and an alert restful state. You may find that if you are sleeping for four hours only, you only deep sleep for ten minutes, and this is to say that you dream for about just ten minutes, and if you are really enjoying your dream you might just reach fifteen minutes. So you would find that out of four hours, only ten and or fifteen minutes is spent on the other reality, after dreaming, you then move to alert restful state in this body you know yourself to be now, you struggle to gain deep sleep, you struggle to remember how to or go back into a dream willingly. But if you could take that very same four hours, and dream for two hours, and then wake up for two hours, you will have found the balance between the four hours. This means that you will be able to wake up for two hours and sleep dream for two hours, you will do this until you realize that you

117

actually sleep into your dreams for two hours, and wake up to what you call your reality for two hours. Only if you will it, only if you will to sleep dream for two hours, and wake for two hours, you will then see that you are actually not sleeping, you will realize that every two hours you keep on moving into and out of different realities that you choose to remember or know yourself to be, and this means that you will have found the balance. You will have found the true way.

The same thing can be said if you sleep for eight hours. If you sleep or spend four hours of that eight in a dream state and the other half into your own little recognized reality, you will also realize that you are not sleeping, you will realize that you are actually breathing, you will see that you are breathing life equally to this side and that side, that side and this side. You will have realized that when you breathe in or inhale on this side, you actually breathe out or exhale that side. Your breath of life will have been equally spread Thato my son. You will then realize another truth, you will see again that you cannot die, and you will then realize that all this time you have forgotten your dreams. You will see that you have killed all your dreams because you have not been breathing life into your dreams by thought. You will realize that, you are the one who has been holding thyself from what thyself wishes and truly desires to be, you will then see that, you have been breathing little amount of breath to that of what you thought yourself being in the future of now. You will then realize that if you really wanted to experience being rich, you could have just slept over it, and you could have just fallen to sleep and just dreamt about it. Right now your system of a day is based on twenty four hours, I tell you this, if you really wish, if you really desire, and finally I can say if you really will it, you can fall into deep dream state for a good twelve hours, if you really believe all of this, only if you choose to do all of this, then you could and would wake for a good twelve hours, then shall ye see where I am, and where I am is where you are right now. I know all of this because I remember where I am.

Iyoh, that was deep!
Yah hey, tell me about it, that is what I thought when I told myself this. I could not believe it, just as you do not believe it Thato my son.
And who told you all of this?

You told me this Thato, remember that you are talking to yourself here. Yah, I have acknowledged, accepted and understood that when I started these notes from the first page, I knew that this was to be about my understanding of the things that make me as I am now.

I tell you this, you should look for the balance if you truly wish to be all of this, you should be that which you truly desire my boy.

Oh… I tell you this, once you find the balance, you will see no suffering, you will see no poverty, you will see no struggle but the choice that a person has thought of and remembered from imaginative memory. You will see how long and how of what people dream and perceive themselves to be. You will understand that it is all a choice of a long thought of thy self. You will understand that, that which you call poverty is a choice, but in a sense it is not, it is just merely an experience, it all depends on how long you dream your experience of thought, it all depends on how many hours you spend now as you know yourself than that which you dream about or to be. It all depends how long you dream yourself being poor, or how many days will ye be poor, how many months will ye be poor, how many years will ye be poor?

Wow… wow… wow I cannot believe this, well I mean I can but… but… but just cannot sink it in man. It is not easy for me to accept this, and I mean if it is that easy, that simple, that quick and fast, then why have I wasted my time on work? What is the point then? Why am I still working if I can just dream myself being rich? What is going on here?

Lol, lol, lol, lol…. I tell you this!

You know why?

Yes that is what I want to know!

It is because someone is dreaming about you working for them, and it is just simply because you are also dreaming of working for someone and fulfilling someone else's dream, remember what a shared thought is, you are sharing thoughts. That someone recognized his or her dream. They dreamt their riches, they know how to dream rich, they know how to follow riches… in order for their dreams to be true, you had to fulfill them, you had to submit yourself and agree to their dreams in the all shared thought of imaginative memory. You do this, and the only way you do this is that because you see, dream and breathe to a thought of yourself

119

working for someone else's dream to fulfill their dream of imaginative thought of memory.

But what else am I supposed to do? I mean the only way of being rich is to have money, and the only way to have money is to work for that which you choose and want to be.

Hah! I have just told you throughout these notes that you are just dreaming, I told you that if you truly want to be rich, just dream about it, and I mean go to sleep and wake to riches now, wake up now Thato my son. Oh my love of my breath, oh my sweet all sweet Thato wake up! Wake up and sleep now, now sleep and wake up! Wake up, sleep, wake up, sleep, wake up and sleep to whatever it is that which you wish to be, and remember to and find your balance. Become the balance, see the balance, see it, breathe it, remember it, imagine it all and understand it, all of it! And then ye shall see thy self.

If you choose wealth, dream wealth and you shall have it. You see, just as you have been doing all this time Thato, you have forgotten or you have chosen to forget that which you truly chose to be. You told me that you once wanted to become a well renowned famous scientist, you also told me that you wanted to become a rapper... in order for you to be all that you want to be, in order for you to be a rapper and for people to understand that which you talk about, you had and have to put yourself in a position of learning a language that people understand, you choose to start as small as a birthed baby and learn all the ways of that one particular constructed language so that people you are trying to impress and entertain may understand that which you are communicating. The same thing can be said of a scientist, he or she also chooses to start as an infant to learn the ways of that which you call a human being. After understanding what this is, the person then remembers his or her dream then thus fulfills it. He or she fulfills it by learning the dream of humans. You as a human believe in math, science, religion, and all of that which is next...in order for you to become a true great scientist you would have to learn all the great things that the other scientist have imagined to be just like Einstein.

Wait a minute here. You just wait! What do you mean by me as a human, I thought you said you are me?

Yes I am you, and I call myself that which I choose to be. And right now I choose to call myself that which I am, right now I choose to call myself

Thato Motchello the human, and I love that name, it has a good twist to it!

Lol, Yah me too hey, I love it so, so much man. And I can change it if I do not like it.

Exactly!

Then I will be whatever I choose to be.

Exactly our point my son, exactly my point Thato.

Okay cool, I get you.

But now, you do not have to take the long way to reach your dreams, you do not have to take the long route about it. If you truly remember, if you truly, truly remember that you do not have to be an infant from start, if you remember how to dream, if you remember how to breathe life into your thoughts or dreams of imaginative memory, you will see how easy it is. You will see the no need for work, and you will just move in, move out and about yourself as you choose for yourself to be, as you have thought yourself to be. Just sleep and wake up between the two or more of your created aspects in a balanced way.

So dreams do become true!

Yes, that is why you would say, "It is a dream come true!"

I am not saying that you should not work, all that I am telling and saying to you right now is that do all that it is you truly desire, do it now and do not doubt it because as much as it is not real it is all possible for that fact! It is all possible because you imagine it to creation from you memory.

So yah, just find the balance and be the balance of dreams and reality. It is that very easy, it is that very easy if you believe all of this, it is that very easy only if you will all this right here now Thato my father. Yes, you get to choose, you get to decide! Now take your pick, you can choose all that which you desire.

Hhhhhaaaaaammm…. Now I feel like praying.

I tell you this, you have been praying all your life, you have been praying every second, every moment and every now. Every thought that you have become and thought about, every single thought you could imagine yourself thinking is your prayer. Your thoughts are your desires, and your thoughts are that which you pray for. You have thought bad things about others, and thus has bad things happened to them, and that is why you have thus prayed bad things on to them. You have thought of jealousy towards someone and thus have you desired all bad things for that person whom you are jealous for and of, and so as it is with your desires, and your desires are the things you pray for, and the things that you pray for are your thoughts, and your thoughts are your imaginative memory. You have desired and wished the best for someone and for yourself, and so as it is with your desires, and your desires are the things that which you pray for, and the things that which you pray for are your thoughts, and your thoughts are your imaginative memory.

I tell you this, many have been cursed in churches.
Many have been cursed in closed bedroom doors and in plain sight.
I tell you this, many have been blessed in churches.
Many have been blessed in closed bedroom doors and in plain sight.
Because a prayer is that which you truly wish and desire, and what you wish for is what you think, and what you think is that which you imagine to be in your memory. And so as you truly believe, so shall it be that you hope on.
Iyoh, thank you for telling me all of this, to be honest with you, I also try not to be jealous of anybody, I mean, well I do wish for some of the things they may poses, but I see no need for me to wish and seek all that is bad towards them. I wish you all the best, I wish for all of you peace, and I wish for your salvation, may you save yourself from thyself as thy self knows itself to be. Be blessed my people, truly yours, Thato Motchello. I love you all, and I am no different from me or you. I am here right now, I am with you here. And this is who I am.
Thank you, thank you so much Thato for giving me all this information, Thank you father Thato, Thank you young Thato for making all this understandable according and towards me as Thato.
Thank you!
So you are saying that in order for me to be my own boss, I have to kill the thought of me working for someone? If I want and choose not to work, I must just think of it from my imagination and fall right into it by deep sleeping into dream state?
If that is what you want then that is how you should choose it to be. So far you have already placed your thoughts in one direction, you have concentrated your thoughts to some routine, you know already that every day when you wake up, you have to go to college, after college you do

work and or your family. This you have thus programmed as a path for your success, in that very same path you still have placed thoughts of doubt of what if you do not make it, what if you do not get a job after finishing college and or save money for or after a while for your retirement? I tell you this, you do not need a job to live, all you need is life! And you can create it by imagining it.

Okay, I get you again. All that I have to do is to choose to deep sleep into dream state now instantly into whatever I want and choose to be, and balance my choices. Or I could imbalance it, and spend a lot of hours or a long time, going to school, and or work to get to where I choose to be. Yes my son, it is that simple, it is that easy. It is that easy only if you choose it.

Okay, I do understand. Thank you once more.

No thank you once more for calling out to yourself. Thank you for remembering me as you Thato. I love you.

Now remember this.

I will remember.

Yah you better.

Lol, stop it man.

You see, you have to or should, only if you wish, open your thoughts to every possible thought of your thoughts. You have chosen to make balance confusing and impossible to can truly understand. In all your confusions and lack of understanding balance, you also know and say that, you need to balance your diet, your sleep, exercise, work and pleasure and all that you can make up. To can confirm this, you now say in your language that too much of a good thing is bad, and this could also mean that too much of a bad thing is good. Because when you do bad for a very long time, you get tired of it and thus move and change to that which you call good. This is why a murderer or a killer can be a killer for this or that long period. And also when you do good for a very long time, you get tired of it and thus move or change to that which you call bad. So once you understand balance, you will not only apply it in your sleep dream state and your reality, but also in everything that you do. In order for you to can feel and be hate, you first have to love. You cannot hate somebody, someone, something or anything before loving it first, and you cannot love something before hating it first. So you might ask yourself, so which one comes first? I tell you this, it is the love for all that you are. It is your love hate, and your hate love towards that particular thing, it is your love for hate. And this is how you love everything all the same. I can only say I love you because I did not like you before, and I can only say I hate you because I loved you before. And all of this can be very confusing and misunderstood because you imbalance it.

Once you find the balance between and for hate and love, you will feel Nothing at all but the balance. When your food is prepared, and there is too much salt, spice, sugar and so forth, you say it is good but there is too much of this or that, and you also say that it could have been better if the flavors and taste were balanced. Now I tell you this, Balance your love hate to anything and you will see and realize how much you actually care and love that person, thing, anything or something. You will see how neutral your feelings will be, you will be okay with that person, thing, something or anything because you will love and hate, hate and love, and once you realize the balance, you will see that, you know what? I am actually okay with this person, thing, anything or something. You will feel Nothing but the feeling you are feeling, and what you are feeling is exactly what you are feeling, just like I have been telling you throughout these notes. Your feelings will be the same, hate will be felt as love and love will be felt as hate, and eventually you will feel neither because it will all be one thing. Once something, anything or anybody is one, it will not identify anything else but refer to itself as that which it is. You see, one cannot refer to itself as two, and also one knows that he, she or it cannot add itself to itself because there is only it.
I see, wow. This is getting too much for me now.
Yah, hhhhmmmmm…. I know, I know.
Now look at this. When you take a classic scale, and weigh two objects on it, let us say that one side is heavier than the other one. In order for you to balance it, you need to put the same amount of weight on the other side equal to the other side, and once it is equal, once it is balanced, there will be no heavy side, all sides will be the same, even if it is of different objects, both will be equal. This means that one side will have the same weight as the other one side, now if they both have the same equal weights, so which one is heavier? I tell you this, none of them is heavy, because none is heavier than the other. In order to can have something

heavy, you need that which is not heavy. Now I can tell you this, if you are truly balanced, if you are truly well balanced, you will not feel a thing, you will not feel pain, suffering, sicknesses, hate, love, struggles and all that you can imagine, you will feel Nothing because there is Nothing out there but you. You are the one who is causing the imbalance and the true balance whenever you choose to.

So go ahead and balance this, and see if you can balance that. Balance that and see if you can balance this. Be the balance. You call yourself a human being, I tell you this, once you understand this, once you understand what and who you are, once you believe all of this, you will have known thyself. And I have told ye of thyself. When you first started out on these notes, you said you wanted to know who you are and what your capabilities are as a human being. And I have told you of whom you are, and your capabilities are limitless to your thoughts of imagination of memory. Once you understand this, you will believe this. Once you believe this, you will know who you are. And once you know yourself, you will know the other person as well because he or she is the same as you. You are not special than anyone or anybody or anything, you are all the same. You feel pain, I feel pain, we all feel pain. I see you, you see me, we all see each other now. Because now you understand yourself, you will understand the next person because they are just as the same as you are. You are not different, this is what you are all experiencing!

You see, once you understand this, once you understand that all I have said here, you will have wisdom. Once you understand that the only way to know yourself is to remember the younger or smaller you, and once you understand that the only way to know yourself is to remember the older or bigger you, you will have understood. Once you understand and realize how small or young you were, you will know because it was and is you. Once you understand who you were and are, you will realize and see no point of it all, you will see no point of it because it was and is you, I mean why would you try to find out who you are? And only to find out who you are! And once you see no point, once you make no sense of what you have made sense of and of what you have gathered of yourself, you will find that you have found yourself. Once you find yourself, you will realize that there is and was Nothing to do.

I told you that understanding is crazy. Because what you are understanding now makes no sense considering that language is all made up, all that you are reading now was made all up. Once you understand that you are already dead alive, you will treasure every moment, you will love every second of that second of that second of moment. You will see every beautiful thing out there. Once you understand how all of you, and I mean all thoughts of you, I mean every thought you thought yourself to be, you will love yourself. You will say hello to yourself every morning.

Okay, I am getting more clarity on all of this one matter.
Man I love your words. Indeed it is all one matter.
So now I would like for you to teach me, show me, and tell me how to do this deep dream state sleep thingy.
I do not have to tell, teach or show you how to do it because you have been doing it already with and without my help. I say this because I am you, and whatever it is that you do, I also do it and have done it. I know this because you have given me the experience of it by thought. You see, every single thought is a frozen continuous dynamic distance. Every thought is already out there waiting to be felt and experienced again. If you already think and thought of yourself being a millionaire or a billionaire, a rapper, an actor, a writer or an astronaut or anything you can think of, that thought is already waiting for you. The question is how you will go about in being that thought again, how long will you take? You can think of things that could help you get there or choose and decide to never get there at all again, you see it all depends on what you will choose from all forms of thoughts you have ever thought about.
Yes, yes, yes I hear what you are saying. And my question is how do I get to any dream that I want and choose to be?
And my answer is... sleep into it.
How? How do I do it?
Mmmmhhhhhhhhh...... I tell you this.
You see, what confuses you, is that you choose to sleep and wake to whatever you want at your will of command. And so far your will was and has and also is passed down on to you by your choices of thoughts experienced with others like you.
So you simply mean that what I am now, I have thus been taught?

Yes because you chose to remember being a thought that is taught in you imaginative creative memory.

Okay, I see you are reminding me here.

Oh yes indeed, you forget quick. The best I can do is to remind you.

So you are still explaining to me how to get to my dreams quick.

Oh yes, I also almost forgot.

You are being funny because I know you did not forget.

Nope I did not, just keeping some smiles back on to faces, you were getting tired there for a moment.

Well you are doing a good job at it, so please tell me more.

Oh I will remind you more.

I remind you this!

What confuses you, like I have said, is that you choose to sleep and wake to whatever you want at your will of command.

I still do not understand what you mean by this.

Okay, I will get into deeper details now. When you wake up in the morning or afternoon to go to work, church, school, college, meeting, or to an entertainment event, you will not choose to sleep there or during the course of that event.

Now from what I have mentioned above, I will select work as a real example. And I will ask you a few questions of which I already have answers to, just to bring you to an awaking or realization. Now I ask you this, would you sleep at work?

Well, yes and no. I say this because I can sleep on my lunch break or and if I do not have a lot of work on my hands I could steel an hour or so just to take a quick nap.

Great answer, I was expecting it. So now would you sleep at work when you have a deadline in the next hour and your work is not finished? Would you sleep while it is still busy at work and you are supposed to serve a customer or a client? Would you leave a live broadcasting presentation on TV and go sleep on the spot? Would you stop your teaching or lecture to students just to go and sleep on the spot? Would you stop your preaching to the congregate just because you only want to sleep? Would you leave a battle field of war and go to sleep on the spot?

What I am asking and telling, is that:

127

A chef does not decide or choose to leave his kitchen while a restaurant is full and busy just to go and sleep because he feels sleepy and tired.

A surgeon does not decide or choose to stop an operation just to go and sleep.

A waiter does not decide or choose to stop service just to go and sleep.

A pilot does not decide or choose to sleep during a course of a flight just to go and sleep!

And now I ask again. Would you stop doing what you are doing during the course of your work hours and go sleep?

Well, I do not think so. I mean no, I would not sleep while I am working and still at work or busy. I mean my boss will rid of me on the spot.

I know. You sometimes go to work, and once being at work, you feel and say to yourself that you do not want to work, you say that you do not feel like working and that you just want to be at the beach, party, or clubbing with friends and or maybe have a braai here and there and about, or even go see your family. But you will not just leave, you will not just walk out of work because you feel like not working on that day of moment. You will not leave because you have created strong thoughts that your job or work you are doing now is providing and giving you money to afford yourself as you would choose. Since you do not wish, want and choose to lose your job, you then despite aside your feelings and decide to remain at your work for that day, and decide that you will later resume to that which you felt like doing on that day when you are working on your off day.

And that my friend is your biggest confusion and an enemy to your dreams. You see, if you really wanted to fall into your dreams, you would sleep anywhere and at any place at any moment. You would stop your work doing at that moment of instant and sleep on the spot. But because for you, the only place you can sleep properly with little or without disturbance is in at your house or room or your comfortable space, so you rather choose to do what pays you first, you are scared to lose your job.

And remember that the only reason you would want to sleep, is because you would want and choose to wake another different life of you up, and in order to wake a different life, you would have to sleep from where you are, that means you would have to put to rest that which you are doing at any instant moment of time at will to be where you would choose to be.

Remember that when you get tired you feel sleepy, and the reason why you are tired is because you are really tired of or from that which you are

128

doing now at any instant of moment, and the only way to stop that which you do not like is to move away from it, and one of the many only ways to move away from that which you do not like now is to close your eyes from where you are right now and sleep, and when you close your eyes, you see Nothing of that which you did not like, you see only black darkness, and once having your eyes closed for a while, you imagine things or places better or worse than where you are now by thinking of them. Once you imagine things and places by thinking of them, you then fall into to them. Twenty minutes later when you decide to open your eyes and wake up, and only to find that you never went anywhere, you were just thinking while eyes closed and the next thing you fell asleep, and into any one of your thoughts that you thought about. After waking up, you then realize that you never went anywhere, you then realize that you are still here and not there anymore. I tell you this, it is because you have forgotten how to sleep dream long into that which you wish for, and this is because you have been awake and sleep dreaming way far too long on one side of your many created thoughts being of imaginative memory.

Wow...wow...wow. Now that is amazing and shocking to know. I mean I did not know that it is and was this simple to be everything and all that I can imagine myself to be. I mean, let me get this straight. All that I have to do is to simply sleep?
Nope, you do not have to because you are already asleep, and you know that you will sleep tonight, tomorrow night and the night of the other night of the day of now. And this is to say that you are already sleeping and doing what I have just said by choice of willed thought.
Lol, so you are basically saying that, only if I choose to sleep or wake up?
Now I can say yes. Yes!
But now if I sleep all the time, will I not get tired of sleeping?
Nope you will not once you fully understand how to sleep!
Okay I hear you.
Tell you what?
What?
How about I explain this whole dream thingy to you on its own? I mean apart and separate from that which we have here. I will tell you how to manipulate it, and how to enjoy dreams of now forever. So I would suggest that you go and experience it for yourself, go and see every

moment of now as it unfolds before you, go and be now. Be it to understand it, and I will give you more clarity on reality dream or dream reality. Go my son and enjoy, go be yourself and Nothing but you. Remember to take your time, there is no time at all but your now time.
Okay, I am in.
Thanks for understanding.
Sure thing.

And now let us remember!

REMEMBER : There is a true lie.
REMEMBER : You are dreaming all the time.
REMEMBER : There is a shared thought. You share your thoughts with others.
REMEMBER : You dream all the time because you use your imagination.
REMEMBER : And in your imagination lies your deepest dreams.
REMEMBER : All your dreams are a memory.
REMEMBER : You are bored.
REMEMBER : You keep yourself entertained because you are bored.
REMEMBER : You are a thought being of imaginative memory.
REMEMBER : There is communicative relative love.
REMEMBER : Language is made up.
REMEMBER : You are a prophet.
REMEMBER : You can judge all you want, and that which you judge is what you now see.
REMEMBER : You are whatever you call yourself to be.
REMEMBER : You love everyone all the same.
REMEMBER : You are the seer.
REMEMBER : You are breath.
REMEMBER : You shall ever die to live.
REMEMBER : This is who you are.
REMEMBER : There is Nothing to do!
REMEMBER : This is Nothing.
REMEMBER : Nothing!
REMEMBER : That is it.

Now you know all of this.

Go and run fast, run as fast as you can. Go tell the world of who you are. Do not tell them who they are. Tell them about you, tell them about yourself, and if they do not believe that this is you, let them believe that this is not you. You have asked me of what makes you who you are and I have told you who you are. Go tell them my son, go tell them my daughter, go tell them my father, go and tell them. Walk the streets and say this is who I am! Say to the world that you finally understand!
Tell them that you understand Nothing.
Hhhhhhhhhhaaaa..... lol, I just took a sigh!
Mmmhhh... I noticed and I know why you did. But I want you to say it.
Oh well fine then... it is because I understand. Yes I do understand. You have now given me the answer. When I started or when we started on these notes, my first and main question was and is why do I need to need? That was the main reason why all of this happened. I have now realized that I need Nothing!
Yes, you need Nothing and you lack Nothing.
I understand.
You understand what.
Yes!
You understand who.
Yes! What is what, who is what, what is who.
Yes!
Why is that, that is why because why is that.
Yes!
So what is the answer.
Yes!
The answer is by who.
Yes!
Who are you.
You are who.
Yes!
When is now and then.
Yes!
Then that means now is here.
Yes! Then that means here is now.
Lol, yes!
So who are we?

My friend we are who.
Who?
Yes!
So who is who?
I think we must ask who, because he is the only one who knows who.
So we must leave it to who?
Yes! Who knows everything.
So what must I do with this?
What do you think?
Am I talking to myself here?
What do you think?
Okay, I know what I am going to do.
Before you do what you know best, remember that sharing is caring. Remember that you share what you have, all you have is your thoughts, and you have this now with you in your hands. Remember that you share your thoughts, and remember that you love everyone all the same. Remember Bob Marley with one love. Remember that your mother and father love you so much. Remember that I shared this with you, and also remember that I am you. Because you asked me about you, I told you about you and where you are from when you are me, because I remembered where I am and I thus told you where I am and who I am. I told you of whom you are, and this is who you are. And that is it.
Okay, I get you, thank you for reminding me, thank you for me okay?
Sure thing.
Thank you so much for everything, thank you for all of this.
I love you.
Now I know what to do.
I now know that I will give this to who.
Yes I told you this.
And because of this, I know who I am.
I now know that I should share this with who.
Who will know what to do with this.
So who am I?
So I am who.
I am the one who is holding this in my hands now.
I know that I am who.
I am Nothing!

And this is who I am.

www.ingramcontent.com/pod-product-compliance
Lightning Source LLC
Chambersburg PA
CBHW032002080426
42735CB00007B/485